X

Spirit Quest

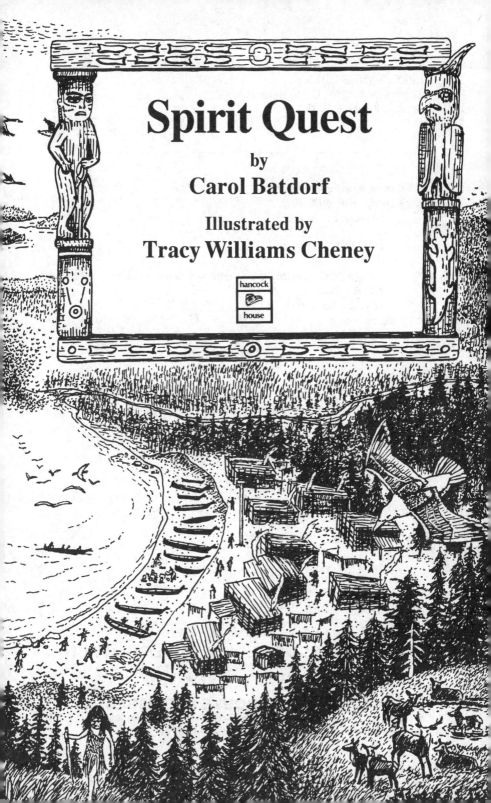

Spirit Quest

by
Carol Batdorf

Illustrated by
Tracy Williams Cheney

hancock
house

ISBN 0-88839-210-9
Copyright © 1990 Carol Batdorf
Second Printing 1997

Cataloging in Publication Data
Batdorf, Carol, 1919 - 1995
    Spirit quest

    ISBN 0-88839-210-9

    1. Cha it Zit, Chief of the Lummi - Fiction. 2. Lummi Indians -
    Fiction I. Title.
    PS3552.A72S64 1990   813'.54   C90-091010-3

Published simultaneously in Canada and the United States by

HANCOCK HOUSE PUBLISHERS LTD.
19313 Zero Avenue, Surrey, B.C. V4P 1M7
(604) 538-1114   Fax (604) 538-2262

HANCOCK HOUSE PUBLISHERS
1431 Harrison Avenue, Blaine, WA 98230-5005
(604) 538-1114   Fax (604) 538-2262

DEDICATION

To Sam and Mary Helen Cagey of Lummi, who, through the years, have been my friends and mentors. Their sharing of insights, information, and stories, and their interest in my personal quest for knowledge of the "old ways" has provided the inspiration to commit what I have learned and felt to paper.

Preface

The year was 1800, approximately, as white men measure time. But the people living along the shores of the island-dotted inlet of the North Pacific, now called the Straits of Georgia, were not of the white race. If they were aware of the existence of humans other than their own kind it was through tales and legends of encounters with strange beings and even stranger spirit canoes long ago. They called themselves "The People" and gave themselves names relating to the territory each group occupied and utilized.

The People in this case were a group who called themselves Lummi. Their domain consisted of a stretch of land along a crescent-shaped bay, a peninsula that jutted, like a boot, into the water at the head of the bay, beaches and hinterland that reached northward for a dozen miles and a number of islands, large and small, that lay to the west in the vast inland sea. All that they needed to live and prosper could be found in abundance in their territory.

They were a proud people, those of the Lummi group, admired by some of the Salish people and hated by others for their aggressions. Ancient traditions, brought to life by myths and legends, formed the backbone of their culture. Personal ambition and achievement was important. Status depended upon the family one was born into, but also upon individual achievement. So, a family, together and as individuals, put forth great effort to excel and to gain prestige through success — to them, success and wealth were synonymous.

Contents

Introduction

Into the household of the *siem*, headman, of one of the villages was born a baby boy. He joined other sons and daughters of Sax ump ki, and his several wives. That boy, and his early life, is the subject of this book. He became the man we know as Cha it zit, chief of the Lummi people during the time of their first contact with white settlers.

Spirit Quest is not historical, in the white society's sense of the word, but it is in the way that *The People* would view it. There are no dates which are not important when one is considering concepts. The details are taken from stories told and re-told from one generation to the next. The scenario is drawn from the value system of those people, from the ways they lived and believed. The narrative is fleshed out by a goodly use of imagination coupled with logic.

Some of the characters are drawn from oral history as it was told to me by elders. Names such as Cha wentz, Sax ump ki and Cha it zit, are historically accurate, others, including Latsi, Wanana, Sta nek, Tselique and Tseutsi, like the characters they portray, are fictitious. We can surmise that such people existed and they have been portrayed as they might have been.

No attempt has been made to present a factual history, but every effort has been expended to create a look at the struggles faced by a Native American boy of Salish origin in his quest for the power necessary for him to assume a viable role in his culture.

 Spirit Quest is written from an Indian point of view, depicting the way events could have taken place, considering the facts as we know them and the culture as it was. The language used is English, but the ideas and thoughts behind the words are Indian. Every effort has been made to reproduce the word-pictures as close to the Native American viewpoint as possible in a language that would have been foreign to them.

Raven

The Test

The boy, Oogli, ran along the mud flats which fringed the great salt water bay, his bare feet splashing through water where the receding tide had left pools.

Clams spurted miniature geysers as his feet pounded the exposed clam beds. The evidence of abundant seafood didn't interest or concern him. That was woman's work. His mission was of greater importance. He held the carved stick which he must deliver clenched tightly in his sweaty hand.

As he sped along, his naked brown body glistening with perspiration, his black hair tangling loosely in a breeze of his own making, he thought of the honor which had been bestowed on him, of the mission of trust and confidence which he had been given. Oogli felt important and he felt humble at the same time. But overriding those emotions was a deep terror, a fear that raced along with him.

In his twelve years the boy who was known only by his pet name "Oogli" had been free to live as he chose. He played at war with the other Indian boys of his village, swam with the seals in the sea, watched the fishermen make their nets and lures. But when his father, headman of his village, handed him the stick, Oogli knew that it would all change. Never again would he be really free.

"Take this stick," his father, Sax ump ki, had said. "Run with it around the edge of the water to the place we call What coom, noisy waters. Follow the river above the falls into the deep woods. When you come to the spot where the river begins, where it departs from its mother-lake, leave the stick where it can be clearly seen. Do not fail in this test, for the spirit forces are watching you. They will know if you are strong or weak, true or false…as will I."

Oogli had realized, then, that the time of his training had begun. He had both feared and anticipated the day when he was considered ready for the ordeal, the preparation for manhood and his spirit quest. If he wasn't equal to the demands that would be put on him, if he failed to receive a true vision—one that would bring them power and guide him through his life—he would be as nothing.

The stick he carried had power, the boy knew. He would need that spirit power to protect him against the evil which dwelled under the dark forest canopy. Even so, the task ahead was perilous. And worse, he thought, was the fact that he must leave the stick and return alone, without its help. Later, he knew, his father would recover the stick, proving that Oogli had actually left it there at the head of the river.

The boy paused for a moment and looked back at his village. Swetquem, as it was called, was situated alongside a creek that emptied into the bay, its longhouses weathered grey from rain and sun. The sight seemed to call to him, "come back where you are safe." He saw slaves on the beach readying canoes for launching while their masters stood by discussing fishing prospects for the day. Village dogs ran excited among them and out onto the tide flats chasing scavanging seagulls. He could hear their distant barking. Then he saw one lone figure standing on top of a small rise behind the houses. It was Latsi, Oogli knew. His sister, always his friend, stood there watching him go.

Reluctantly, Oogli turned and sped on. Soon he could hear the muted roar of the falls, swollen with spring rains as it cascaded over sheets of pot-holed sandstone on its tumble to the bay below. The roar grew in volume and the boy thought of the water spirit that lurked in its turbulence. Then, in a moment, he saw the falls — white, tossing spumes of mist into the morning sunshine. A rainbow trembled in the spray.

Soon he was scrambling up the edges of the slippery rocks as the roiling water grasped at his ankles. Stories shot through his mind, tales told by the village elders of beings who lived in whirlpools and dragged the unwary into the depths never to be seen again.

Underbrush grew thick at the fall's edge, seeming to reach out for the spray that washed over them. There was no escape from the falls, so the boy toiled upward, leaping from rock to rock where he could and facing the water stoically when he was forced to climb. As he reached the top and saw the river running freely, he shouted with triumph.

Overhead, a lazily soaring raven cawed back at him. Oogli recognized the call as a good sign. Raven, one of the most powerful of the creatures, was watching over him. "He who has Raven as a guardian spirit is a fortunate one," the elders would say. "Raven is clever and he has great power."

The river was too deep to wade, and the current was too swift to swim against, so Oogli was forced to push his way through the matted growth along its banks. Salal, berry brambles, stinging nettles and poison spined devil's club barred his way in a disorganized, senseless jungle. Barbs and brambles tore at his flesh and the merciless nettles stung his skin into countless welts. But the boy scarcely noticed the pain he was so intent on his mission.

Beyond the river banks the forest closed in. Giant trees, cedar and fir, reached to the sky and then spread their branches in a cover so dense that it blocked out the sun.

The forest was filled with danger—a place to be avoided. It was there that Tsonika lived, the horrible witch who stole children and took them to her den in a basket. Many times, when the story tellers were recounting ancient legends, he had heard of Tsonika—and always his mother had warned Oogli to be good and not to go near the dark woods behind the village where Tsonika might be hiding.

Oogli pushed on, clasping the stick, hoping for its protective powers to keep him safe. He constantly glanced back and to the sides fearful of what he might see, but not wanting to be taken by surprise. He heard the rustle of wings, such as ravens make in flight, and looked up to see the black bird flying above him. "He is a big one," Oogli thought, "the biggest I have ever seen." Looking up he cawed in the raven tongue and the bird answered.

Reassured, and certain now that the raven was indeed protecting him, the boy gave his full attention to the task of threading his way through the thickets. Ahead the river made a bend. There the current had created a small sand and gravel beach. Suddenly Oogli felt very tired and he slumped on the sand to rest.

Whether he slept or not, he was not sure, but it seemed to him that the raven swooped down and lit on the branch that grew just above his head. It seemed to him, too, that they communed silently, the bird and the boy. A crashing in the underbrush brought Oogli from his reverie. He looked up, startled, to see a bull elk emerge and leap down the low bank. Unaware of the boy, the animal drank from the river. It was not until the elk had wandered back into the forest that Oogli moved. He noticed that the sun was high

14

in the sky, and he had not yet completed the first part of his test.

Rounding the bend, he came upon a large rock walled pool from which the river poured on its descent to the sea. High sandstone cliffs circled it, and a torrent gushed into the pool, falling in a roaring spray of water into a whirlpool that sang its own song of danger. Oogli stared, breathless, at the sight. This was indeed the home of water spirits. Its wild beauty excited him even while it terrified him. "Where is my raven?" he wondered. There was no sight of the bird. "Stick," he addressed the carved wood, "Use your powers to protect me from the evil forces that I can feel here."

Searching for a way around the cliffs, Oogli left the protection of the river and fought his way up the rocks. Soon he was under the forest cover. It was open, but little light penetrated. Up, up he climbed until at last he stood on top of the cliff and looked down into the whirlpool below. Its open maw seemed to draw him—the dizzying height invited him to release himself and to plummet to the water below. Then he heard the raven caw. The spell was broken and Oogli turned to follow the river.

It led him past delightful pools, now surrounded by ferns. Fish darted in the shallows. Sunlight filtered through the trees. He heard the roar that told him of another falls, and soon he came upon it. It tumbled over pot-holed rocks that he could easily climb. Soon he came to the lake his father had described.

The lake seemed to smile on him, sunlight glinting from its rippled surface. Remembering the instructions his father had given him he looked for a flat white stone.

"You will see it lying in a clump of grass at the head of the lake where the river pours out," he had been told. "Place the stick under the rock."

Walking a little farther, he saw the stone and, removing it, he scooped out a hollow, placed the stick in it, and put the stone back on top.

"Stone," he said out loud, "guard this property of my father well that he may know I have done as he asked."

Looking over his shoulder for any danger, Oogli turned downstream knowing that now he had only his own resources to protect him from the spirit presences in the forest which surrounded him. As he beat his way back, following the broken bushes and crushed grasses that he had damaged in his ascent up the river, his senses were keenly alert. More than once he thought he saw black shadows slipping from tree to tree, following him silently. Any noise, the whisper of the wind in the branches, perhaps, or the flutter of a bird's wing, chilled his bones.

"Sasquatch," he thought, that dreaded man-like beast, or beast-like man; he could be hiding near. He recalled how the old women of the village hung hunks of meat in the trees to appease the creature so that it would not harm any of the people. "I have seen them," he recalled hearing his grandmother say. "They are taller, much taller than any man, covered with fur, black with silver tips. One must always be careful of the Sasquatch, especially in the forest," he had been told. The thought pushed Oogli on even faster—past the first falls, past the cataract and whirlpool—stumbling as he flung himself through the bushes—down the turbulent river, falling over the rocks at its edge—and at last to the falls that cascaded over the cliff and into the bay.

That night in the longhouse, Oogli's father called the family together. The evening meal was over and the hearth fire sent lazy curls of smoke drifting toward the hole in the roof. It was the time that Oogli liked best. One could rest on the sleeping platforms warmed by soft furs and a full stomach, or play games with the other young people, or even just sit and talk. Then, too, story tellers offered tales of great events, deeds or ancestors or spirit power.

"Tonight will be special," he thought, for his father, a man to be respected, had something important to say.

Oogli looked at his father with pride showing in his face. Sax ump ki was an impressive figure. Taller than the other men of the village, he carried himself erectly and with confidence.

"My people," he said in the resonant voice he used for special occasions. "I wish to tell you that my son, Oogli, has passed his first test. He has gone alone past What coom while the falls were at their greatest power and has deposited my *cou* stick at a place far into the forest. He has shown courage and truthfulness. He is now ready to begin training. I, as *siem*, headman of these many houses, and other villages as well, have chosen to train him in the ways of manhood. If he succeeds and gains spirit power of his own, I shall name him headman to follow me."

Pride grew in Oogli. He tried to put it beneath him, but it would not stay. He looked at his mother—she sat, hands folded in her lap, her eyes down, but Oogli could see the smile that played about her lips. Then he saw Latsi. She was looking at him, her dark eyes shining and her mouth curled into a delighted grin. Oogli felt that pride rising in him—the feeling that he couldn't quite defeat.

The training began the very next morning, before the blue heron had circled the village, sounding its raucous cry on its way to its fishing grounds. The sky was grey, with just a hint of the dawn to come when, Sax ump ki shook Oogli from sleep.

"Come," he commanded, "it is time for one who would be a man to cleanse himself." Oogli sat up a bit reluctantly, tossing the warm fur robe from his naked body. The early spring air felt cold and damp. His wish was to burrow down under the fur and sleep till the sun called him, but his father's voice gave no opening for resistance.

Running to the salt water was bracing. He could hear his father's feet pounding the path behind him. Oogli was knee deep in the icy water when his father handed him a spruce bough.

"Whip yourself with these. The hurt will strengthen you. From this time on you will know the companionship of pain. But remember that the pain will be your friend. Out of it will come the vision of the spirit power that is awaiting you. When you have prepared yourself, when your own spirit is ready, you will know what *gift* you are to receive."

Oogli took the branch and tentatively felt its stiff, sharp needles. A shiver ran through him as he thought of inflicting them on his flesh.

"It is very important, my son," Sax ump ki continued, "that you listen to the words that I speak. I will only say them one time. It is also very important that you do as you are instructed. If you do not obey and follow the age-old pattern perfectly, a vision and the power it brings may be denied you."

The old man looked at the boy closely. For a moment Oogli met his gaze, but he could not tolerate the intensity which showed through his father's eyes.

"Yes," he answered, "If I fail in my quest I shall never become important. I will be lower than the lowest slave."

"That is true," Sax ump ki frowned at the possibility. "I have chosen you to follow after me, to lead our clan. Do not disappoint me...or our people."

Then with a swift motion, Sax ump ki snatched the spruce branch from Oogli's hand and lashed it across the boy's bare chest. Oogli, taken by surprise, yelped and cringed from the pain.

"A true man never acknowledges pain," Sax ump ki stated with disgust. "That is your first lesson. You reacted as a girl would. Never again do I wish to hear the cry of pain from you. Now, take this branch and inflict it upon yourself."

Reluctantly, Oogli took the branch. The shame he felt hurt more than did the pain. His chest was red where the needles had struck, and dots of blood were gathering in the welts. Then, closing his eyes and stiffening his cold body, he struck himself with the branch. His legs, his arms, his abdomen felt the stinging agony as the needles ripped into his flesh. The pain bloomed and grew until his body was enveloped in it, but Oogli uttered no sound.

"Now," his father commanded, "plunge into the sea."

Oogli hesitated only a moment, thinking of the cold water and the sting of the salt in his wounds. Then he raced to the gently lapping sea and flopped into the water. At first the salt ate deep into his pain, but then the cold numbed him and the sea water seemed to purify him.

The boy felt strangely exhilarated. He felt strength flowing into and through him. He rode on the crest of his pain. It was as if he had risen into a new dimension of being — being that is invulnerable, proud and strong.

"Come out, now," Sax ump ki bade him.

Running to shore, Oogli felt more as if he was flying — somehow looking down on himself.

When they had returned to the longhouse the women had already risen and were laying out the food for the morning meal. Oogli had hoped to avoid being seen in his bloody condition, but Latsi, who had been helping their mother shred dried salmon before placing it in the cooking box, spied the welts as he slipped past her.

"What happened?" she asked, her eyes round with concern.

"It was nothing," he answered. "It's just man's business." Then tossing his bearskin robe over his shoulders, both for warmth and to hide his wounds, Oogli took his place at his mother's cooking fire.

"Here, son," Wanana, his mother, said handing him a piece of dried salmon, "You may chew on this while the rest is softening in the cooking box."

Oogli reached for the morsel, but his father intervened. "Food will soften you," he said. "You must learn to do without. There may be times when there won't be any, then, unless your body is prepared, it will suffer." He took the salmon from Oogli's hand and placed it in the cedar box with the breakfast fish.

Oogli's mother, watching her husband, wondered at his harshness. She knew that Oogli's period of training had begun, but she felt that a slow introduction would serve as well. Even though she knew that it was man's business and a woman had no part in it, her heart cried out for her son.

It was not until evening that Oogli was allowed to eat. And then it was only a small portion of the seafood chowder his mother had made from dried fish, seaweed and powdered, dried clams.

After the meal was finished and the women, Wanana, Tseutsi, who was Sax ump ki's mother, had cleared the hearth, and the other women of the long-house — relatives who tended their own fires — had done the same, Sax ump ki rose to speak.

"My family," he began, "This day my son, who will one day be headman, began his training. It is a hard time for him. We must help him to gain his power. Our own spirit power will assist him...and we must open the way however we can. We must not feel sorry for him," Sax ump ki said, looking directly at Latsi. "We must help him keep to his training so he will be ready when it is time for his quest."

Oogli noticed how Latsi frowned and clenched her small fists. "She is upset," he thought. "I can't let her get into trouble with our father because of me. I think this training will be harder on her than it will be on me. Poor Latsi. I must talk with her."

"Now," Sax ump ki continued, "I call upon all of you...cousins, aunts, uncles, grandmother, grandfather, mother and sister...to help Oogli to observe the demands of this time."

Talking Stick

Spells Of
The Past

The days passed quickly. Oogli was challenged each morning—some new task to perform, some feat of endurance to further toughen his body, strengthen his resolve, and to build his fortitude. He became pale. His ribs showed under his skin, but his muscles were taut and his mind was alert.

One evening, after the hearths had been cleaned and the food boxes put away, Sax ump ki stood before the family group and tapped his talking stick sharply. At the sound, activity stopped and all eyes focused upon him.

"My family," he began in a tone reserved for important announcements. "We all know that we are a proud and a great family. We know, too, that many great men have stood in this place here before we came.

Now it is time for us to pass on the tales of their deeds to the young who are coming up among us. I speak chiefly of my son, Oogli, but there are others here, too — my daughter, Latsi, and the children of my brothers — who should know these things. Tonight Sta nek, my father and the grandfather of the children I speak of, has agreed to tell the ancient stories of our people."

Oogli felt a sense of delight. The old man could weave a spell when he told the tribal stories. One could feel how things must have happened when he spoke. He had a great *gift*, Oogli knew, a gift that could only have come through a spirit quest.

When the withered old man rose from his place on the platform at the head of the huge house and came forward to face the people, the boy noticed how frail he looked. His hair was streaked with white and hung loosely down his back, thin and wispy. A few white hairs formed a sparse mustache which drooped at the edges of his mouth. He held a stout staff, which he leaned on heavily. But when the old man spoke it was in a clear, deep voice, a voice trained and honed by years of story telling.

Sta nek sat on a bentwood box that had been placed near the edge of the platform. For a few minutes he looked off into space — his eyes seeming to look back into time, back to when the world was not as it is — but as it was when all was new. The people waited in silence, knowing that when the mood was right the story teller would begin.

"Long ago," he said at last, "our people lived in another place beyond the waters. They lived much as we do today, but there was hunger in their villages. There was a man — I do not know what his name was — who decided to go trolling for salmon one fall morning, hoping to catch enough fish to feed the people. The autumn leaves were beginning to turn red and gold and he knew that the cold stormy days were coming soon. 'A few more fish to fill the

empty boxes will be good,' he thought. 'Perhaps a wandering spirit will take pity on us and bid the fish to come.'

"He was well into the swift waters that raced by his village when a dense fog, such as often comes in the autumn, engulfed him. Soon he was isolated in a cloud of white. He could see nothing. No sound came to him through the mist.

"'I must do something' he thought to himself, 'or I shall drift out to sea or maybe onto rocks.'

"The thought came to him that the tide was coming in, so if he could follow its flow, he would eventually drift to land and be saved. He needed something light that would float and follow the current, but there was nothing in his canoe that he could toss into the water except his spear, fishing line and paddles.

"'I could sacrifice one paddle,' he decided. So he broke his paddle into small pieces and proceeded to toss them into the water bit by bit. The pieces began to drift in a line and he, using the remaining paddle, followed after.

"Now, at that same time a whale was swimming along with his mouth open, swallowing whatever food he happened to find—fish, squid, skate, it didn't matter. He came to the chips of paddle and, eating them, he followed along until he came to the canoe with the man in it. The whale swallowed them, too.

"Suddenly the fisherman, who hadn't seen the whale because of the fog, was inside the whale, still sitting in his canoe.

"'What will I do?,' he wondered. 'This situation is much more serious than the fog was.'

"He sat there for a long time pondering. At last he moved a bit to be more comfortable. His head rubbed against something soft and warm. Just then the whale coughed. The sound was like thunder and the whale's belly shook, bouncing the fisherman and his canoe about like pieces of firewood.

"'What was that?' he asked himself in great alarm.

"The soft object bounced against his head again and he reached up to feel it. It seemed to be some sort of a sac. He pushed it away. Again, the whale coughed. That gave the man an idea. He reached out and gave the thing a good, hard slap. That made the whale cough so hard that he coughed the man out, canoe and all.

"He looked about. The fog was gone, but nothing looked familiar to him. He was afloat in his canoe near a pine beach. Beyond the sand and gravel bushes heavy with ripe berries tempted him. Beaching his canoe, he began to explore.

"There were clams thick in the stones and under the sand. Clam holes were visible everywhere he looked, up and down the shore. Above the beach, beyond the bushes, he could see open meadows where deer were grazing. In the background giant trees grew, and over all was a towering mountain.

"'It is a good place,' he thought, 'There is plenty of food, trees for a lodge, and from that mountain I could see any enemy approaching. Since I don't know where I am, or how to find my village, I shall be content here.'"

Sta nek paused. "That is how our people came," he told them. "He was our ancestor. His village became known as Al lu lung.

"For many years…longer than we can imagine…our people prospered and grew in numbers. When there were too many some spread out to the other islands.

"Always there was plenty of food, fish in the sea around them, clams waiting to be dug, and all manner of other sea foods. There were berries to be picked: salal, salmonberries, blackberries, huckleberries, and high on the mountain, blueberries. But best of all were the soapberries. Just like us, the people relished the frothy soapberry desserts the women made.

"But as the islands filled with descendants of that first man they began to look toward the mainland that they could see in the distance. The village headmen sent warriors out in their large war canoes to explore along those distant shores. They found people living in longhouses similar to their own in small villages such as they themselves built. Gradually the people began to visit back and forth and to trade among themselves.

"So it happened that a young Lummi man by the name of Swallochk saw and desired a girl who lived with her people at a village which was called Momli, which lay where a river empties into a pleasant bay along the mainland.

"After a courtship and the proper exchange of gifts, the young man was invited to move into the bride's home and live with her family. Since her family was an important one and the longhouse was large, he accepted the arrangement rather than take the girl to his own family's home.

"Swallochk's wife was all that he could desire. She was industrious and pampered his every wish. All of this attention served to spoil him and he began to think of himself as being quite important.

"At last the time came when nothing she would do pleased him and he began to become insulting to her. One day he told her that she was getting fat and ugly. 'Your legs are so heavy that they resemble fat fish,' he flung at her.

"After that," Sta nek continued, "her brothers heard her sobbing and asked her what was wrong. Then she told them how her husband had begun to abuse her. The brothers were very angered at this and they demanded that the young man return to his village.

"So, having no choice, he went home in disgrace. As the days passed in the home of his parents he began to regret the way he had acted and wanted to return to his wife and the comforts of her house. His parents encouraged him in this for they didn't want trouble with her tribe and they disliked seeing their son the cause of it.

"So one morning, taking his younger brother with him to act as negotiator, Swallochk paddled across the waters to the mainland. The tide was out when they arrived at Momli, so they had to beach the canoe some distance from shore in the mud flats.

"Their approach had been noticed by his wife and her brothers and they decided to make short work of him. Since his departure, his bride had considered herself lucky to be rid of such an inconsiderate husband and had no wish to have any further contact with him. So they devised a plan.

"Meanwhile Swallochk, having to leave the canoe on the mud flats, told his brother, Whathum, to stay with it and to watch it. He was sure his wife would be delighted he had returned so his brother's presence would not be necessary. In fact, he could see her running toward the beach even then.

"When he reached the pebbly beach she greeted him fondly, and invited him to sit with her on the ground to discuss their life together. He reclined beside her and gently she pulled his head onto her lap. Then she entwined her strong fingers through his long hair. Her brothers, who had been hiding behind, leaped out and quickly dispatched him.

"From the flats the younger brother who had watched the entire proceedings leaped into the canoe and streaked for Al lu lung before they could pursue him and murder him, too.

"On his way home he vowed to avenge his brother's death. From that time on he dedicated himself to acquiring such powers that he would be invincible against those people.

"First, he climbed the highest point on the mountain above Al lu lung. There he fasted and sought a vision that would reveal where he would find the source of this power. All he heard was the wind sighing, 'It isn't here.' Then he dove into the lakes on the island, but the sound of his own blood rushing through his head told him, 'It's not here.'

"At last he tied rocks to his feet and dove into the waters of the swift, cold water of the straits that boiled past his island — the deepest water known to his people. He dove and he dove until he was exhausted, but he could find nothing. At last, when he cared neither whether he would live or die, he dove one more time. Then, between life and death, in the cold, dark water, he heard a voice say, 'What you seek is in a lake near your home.'

"So, he returned to his village. In the lake that lay almost at the entrance to his family's house he found a club lying on the bottom that was like no other he had ever seen. 'This is the source of your power,' a voice told him. 'With it you will be as a hundred men.'

"When Whathum returned to Al lu lung and told them what had happened and showed them his mighty gift, he said, 'Let us avenge my brother. Follow me and together we will defeat the enemy.'

"That is how it happened that early one morning a group of war canoes slid out of the long, finger-like harbor near Al lu lung and headed for Momli.

"When they arrived, the warriors leaped from their canoes and raced ashore, Whathum in the lead, brandishing his mighty club. Screaming war cries, they slaughtered everyone in sight. At last they approached the longhouse of an old man, a mighty *siem*. He beseeched them to cease their butchering.

"'You have proved your might,' he cried. 'You have avenged your brother's murder. If you will spare my family and me, since we are all that are left, I will give you all the lands we held up to the point where the branches of the river meet. There we will go to live and will never menace you or in any way seek to do you harm.'

"Whathum was tired, his anger was gone, and he was happy to let the old man and his family go in peace. Since the land was rich and the buildings were good, that is where he decided to remain."

The old man, Sta nek, seemed drained. His shoulders sagged and his lined face appeared pale and haggard. He looked at his family gathered about him. For a long time no one spoke. Oogli began to stir restlessly, but he knew better than to speak or to leave. His grandfather was away in his thoughts and would return when the stories had quieted in his mind.

After a long silence, when no one spoke, Sta nek aroused himself. "My people," he said, "You are the descendants of Whathum and the others who chose to leave Al lu lung and come here, first to Momli and then to other villages around our beaches. Now we are powerful, we have much land on which to hunt and many islands from which to fish and gather food. All the tribes look at us with respect. Always carry yourselves with honor and dignity. I speak these words so that the young in our midst will hear them. I speak them especially to Oogli who is becoming a man, and if he proves himself, may someday be a leader of our people."

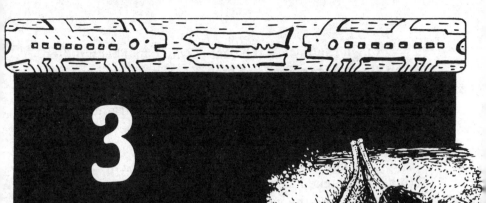

3

The Challenge

"It is time you learned the ways of
the sea," Sax ump ki said to Oogli one
morning later in the summer. "I have seen
you practicing, pretending that you were a master
of the canoe. Now you must become one. Do you see my
small traveling canoe on the beach?"

"Yes," Oogli answered.

"Take it. Go to the island at the head of the bay
where you will find what is waiting for you. If you are wise,
you will turn this challenge into a benefit to yourself."

The boy wondered at his father's words, but had
learned not to question the meaning. It would reveal itself
in time. Instead he answered, "I have had no breakfast, and
I will need some berry cakes to eat on the way. Let me fill
my stomach at the fire and then I will go."

"No," Sax ump ki replied sternly. "I thought you had
learned that a man can withstand hunger, as he can pain. If
you are to be a man of any account you must learn that
lesson. Go now!"

Oogli ran toward the canoe, which had been pulled up on the beach above the high tide line. The boat was sturdy, built with a high prow to travel easily through the turbulent tide-rips of the vast inland sea. He strained at the anchor rope, inching the craft down into the water. His father watched, but made no effort to help.

"A man must learn to do for himself," Oogli's thoughts mimicked what his father might have said. At last the boat slid into the water and the boy leaped into it. He grabbed a paddle to steady the rocking canoe and pushed out toward the distant island.

The island lay just inside the long channel which gave entrance to the crescent-shaped bay where the village stood. Oogli had been there before, only then it was different. As he paddled toward the mist-shrouded purple-grey outline of the island he remembered how his mother had called to him one morning—it seemed so long ago. "Come son," she had said, "We will travel and gather food." It had been exciting, then, with provisions piled high around him. Latsi was only a baby and she rode strapped to her cradle board. Oogli had tilted the board so Latsi could see all around her. He felt safe and secure, feeling the strong impulse of his father's paddle behind him, and watching his mother in the prow pulling her paddle with ease. That was so long ago when Oogli was still under Wanana's protective care. He ached now for her gentle touch—a touch which he had noticed these past months had carefully been withheld.

His musings carried him back to those more comfortable days. He recalled how the family, just his father and mother and he and Latsi—not the three other wives and their children—had loaded their large traveling canoe. He had helped Wanana load the cattail mats, bundles of dried food, drying spits and digging sticks. Then he had watched while Sax ump ki put in his fishing and hunting gear—nets, lines, hooks, spears, bows, and all the necessities of the chase. When it was done, his father had said, "Now, Oogli." He had jumped in and found a place among the baggage.

Then his mother had taken her place at the helm, ready with her paddle, and Sax ump ki had shoved them off, running and leaping into the stern.

Oogli remembered the sensation as his father's strong arms sent them out into the calm waters of the bay. He remembered, too, how Sax ump ki had sung his power song as he and Wanana kept to the beat, dipping, pulling — dipping, pulling. The song had a magical quality, he knew, giving strength and protection to its owner-singer. Oogli could not sing the song. No one could except he to whom it was given. Even then, as a precaution, the real meaning was hidden. The words were only hints of the real power of the song.

Now, paddling by himself across those same waters, Oogli wished the song was his. His arms and back began to ache from the strain of the constant motion and the wind was beginning to rise, churning the bay into an angry chop. He could remember the song very well, for he had heard it many times before. He remembered those times in the longhouse during the winter celebrations when his father's spirit came upon him and he leaped into the circle to dance. Then the drums had picked up the beat of the song and everyone sang it together. It was an exciting, scary time, he recalled. Then the spirits were there, and it was dangerous. Any mistake in the words or dance could spell deep trouble.

"Will I get a spirit song?" he wondered. "What would it be?" When he was ready and went out on his own spirit quest — would he succeed? Some didn't, he knew and they became nothing, no-account people. Some even died while trying. Worse yet, Oogli thought, was to get a poor spirit that had no power to help its owner.

On and on he went, fighting the wind and the water, straining to reach the island that seemed to be slipping farther and farther away. In his ordeal, alone with forces that could destroy him, Oogli came to the awful realization that his entire life, his place in the clan, his future prosperity and prestige lay in successfully completing his quest for spirit power. There would be no one to help him. He saw then that his father, who seemed so harsh, was really trying to prepare him for the terrible challenge that awaited him. Little by little Sax ump ki was introducing him to the rigors that must be met and mastered.

"From now on I will try even harder," Oogli vowed. Then he remembered how he and his family had landed on the beach of the island. "We will stay here a while and gather food from the sea," his father had said.

The thought of food brought pangs of pain to Oogli's abdomen. "I must not think of food," he reminded himself. "It is a weakling who travels on his stomach."

The hours passed — minutes counted by the steady cadence of the boy's paddle. The wind began to freshen and whitecaps tossed bits of froth across the water. Overhead, tendrils of clouds scurried across the sky — a sky that began to darken. Worried, Oogli pushed his tired body, "I must get to the island before the storm strikes," he told himself.

It seemed to him that during the long hours he had been paddling the island had retreated before him. Never did it grow any bigger but always it was there, half hidden in mist, no closer than before.

The wind had risen alarmingly. Oogli's canoe wallowed in the troughs and then sprang to life when a wave rose under it, but he was too exhausted to be frightened. Then the boy noticed a strange thing. Something seemed to be guiding the canoe. It moved steadily, almost smoothly, cutting through the waves, and the island appeared to be moving closer, coming rapidly toward him.

"A spirit of the sea...it is helping me," Oogli cried aloud, his mind as confused as his body was sore. He felt that he was drifting in a dream world not really in the surging, bobbing canoe but suspended somewhere above it. "Whatever is happening, do not be afraid," a voice seemed to be saying to him.

How long he remained in a dream state, Oogli did not know, but he was jarred into consciousness when he felt the canoe crunch on a stony beach. Somehow he found the strength to pull the craft onto the shore before he fell to the ground. How long he lay there, pressed flat against the beach gravel, Oogli didn't know either. When he opened his eyes the sun was low on the horizon and the storm clouds were tinted with the colors of sunset.

When he struggled to get up he felt a strange thing. A blanket covered him and his head rested on a sleeping mat. Then he saw the old man. He was sitting on a drift-log not ten feet away.

Oogli was startled and then appalled by the stranger's appearance. He seemed to be more of an apparition than a living person. His hair, which was a strange shade of red mixed with grey, hung down his back and draped over his shoulders in matted strings. He was naked except for a loin cloth and an amulet of carved bone which hung from a thong about his neck. His body was a rack of bones, so emaciated that every rib was clearly visible and his skin seemed to have been stretched tight over it all.

"How thin he is," Oogli thought. "Food must be very scarce. But then, I am thin, too. I wonder who, or what he is."

"Ho," the old man said, "I see that the boy brought by the sea awakens."

"I was sent here by my father, Sax ump ki...and a storm came up...I was so tired..." Oogli tried to explain,

35

but his words would not come out right and his own voice sounded far away.

"I know," the man said. "Come, I have food for you. When you have eaten and rested, then we will talk."

Oogli rose, his head reeling, and followed the elder up a short trail to a house which was moldering with age. Inside the old man stirred a small, smoky fire, feeding bits of wood until it burst into flames. Then he opened a bentwood cooking box and took out a piece of freshly barbecued salmon. The aroma set Oogli's mouth to watering, and he eyed the fish hungrily.

"Here is some salmon, freshly caught. It is still warm from the fire," the old man said as he handed it to Oogli. "Don't eat too fast...nor too much. I fear that your stomach will refuse to take it if you rush, for you have been without food for a long time."

When Oogli had eaten and rested he began to wonder about this strange old man. Had his father known that he would be there? Was there a reason for all that was happening? Was this a part of his training? Most of all he wondered who or what the old man was. Was he a person at all—or maybe he was a spirit or some superhuman being. He marveled at the fact that he felt no fear of the man, only curiosity. He was so strange. Was he a shaman? If so, Oogli knew that he must be very careful, for shamen had great powers—powers to cast spells, to even kill.

"You are wondering about me," the old man said, as if he had read Oogli's thoughts. "I mean you no harm. I knew of your coming. You are of my lineage. Your father is my nephew. It is I who trained him as he is now training you. There is much that you should know if you are to be a leader of your people. Events of the past cast a shadow over happenings of today. A wise man takes all things into consideration when he sets the course of his people. Listen well to what I have to tell you."

Oogli looked at the elder solemnly, realizing that what he was about to hear was important and that it would not be repeated. He settled back comfortably against the cooking box and waited for the old man to begin.

Time passed, the sun drew close to the edge of the sea, but the strange old man sat quietly, staring into space, it was as if his soul had left his body. Then, he roused himself, stirred the fire, studied Oogli's face intently, but did not speak.

Finally Oogli could not deny his curiosity. "Are you a shaman?" he asked, a little frightened at his own question.

"You could say so," the old man answered with a hint of a smile hovering around his thin lips. "I have certain powers which I will use against my enemies if I have the chance. I can speak with the dead—I have often visited them in the village of the dead. But I can also heal, and retrieve the souls of those who are yet living but who have had their souls snatched from them. But I will not harm you. My purpose is to instruct you. I will give you my name, but you must not speak it in the presence of others, for there is power in a name, and mine is most potent. My name is Tselique.

"There are many things known to me," the shaman said. "Some of them I will not speak of, for they might harm you if you knew of them. But there are others that should be known by the son of a great chief. If you, yourself are to be great and honor your lineage, you must be wise. Your wisdom and knowledge must stand above that of the common man. For that reason I will speak to you of supernatural things. Keep these things in your mind, Oogli, for some day you may need knowledge of them."

Oogli nodded, fearing to speak and break the trend of the old man's thinking, or appear to be presumptuous.

"Many years ago—beyond the memory of our elders, or even of those who went before them—strange

37

beings came to our place. It has been told that there arose from the horizon a huge white spirit, with many wings carrying it more swiftly than any canoe toward our village. It came across the sea silently, followed by hundreds of sea gulls, as if they were serving the needs of the spirit. Before long a second spirit appeared far out at sea and moved toward the land as quietly and rapidly as the first.

"The people who were watching it became frightened and ran into the forest to hide. Even the warriors and the chief feared to face this spirit visitor. The two spirits drew close to the shore and then a strange thing happened. Beings appeared and ran about inside the spirit. They caused the white wings to be folded in such a way that they lay crosswise on posts, and the spirit was seen by the people as a skeleton form. The people watching were terrified at the vision they had seen and wondered what great power they were witnessing.

"After that the beings lowered heavy canoes from the belly of the spirit into the water and paddled to shore, except that they did not paddle at all, but seemed to propel themselves in a magical way. When they had landed the people could see that those alien creatures were white. Yes, their skin was white and their eyes were pale. Their hair was strange, too, pale in color, and some was twisted strangely. When they walked, they rolled clumsily. They were tall — giants. Their clothes were strange, not at all suited to our climate. Some wore hard looking caps, and stiff shirts, but strangest of all were their feet. They were not like feet at all, but were black and stiff-looking, which might have accounted for their rolling gait. I do not know — I only know what I have been told.

"The beings made strange noises among themselves. No one could make any sense out of their mutterings. They went into the houses of the villages. When they came out the people could see that they were carrying many fine pelts and fur robes. No one dared to challenge them, since they did not know what magic power the aliens might possess. Later others came in from the spirit and brought large containers which they filled with water from a nearby stream. The beings went about taking whatever they wanted — carved boxes and trays, spears, woven blankets, even small canoes. When they had taken all they wished for, they put it all in their canoes and paddled back to the spirit.

"The frightened people watched as the beings caused the white wings to raise themselves and the spirit began to slowly move and then to ride across the water. Soon the second spirit followed after and all was as it had been before except that the villagers were left without their most precious belongings.

"The chief sent messengers to other villages, telling of the terrible, frightening thing that had happened. Soon other runners appeared from distant villages with a report of the same thing happening to them. All up and down the coast the villages had been robbed, and worse yet, some of their young women had been accosted and abused, even stolen away.

"At last the elders of the villages held council and decided that the evil spirits must be dealt with. 'If we all join together' they said 'Our power will be great, perhaps even greater than the spirit power of the beings. We cannot tolerate this marauding any longer. We shall see who is greatest.'

"So a great army was formed. Scouts watched the movements toward the ancient Lummi village. All the warriors, under the leadership of Ractamoos, a renowned Nisqually war chief, hastened toward that point.

Ractamoos placed his seasoned warriors in the thick forest behind the village. All day they waited until late in the afternoon the spirits entered the bay. The army waited while the beings, carrying heavy *sticks* came to shore in their large, heavy canoes to get water. Then, while the beings were engaged, Ractamoos gave the order and the entire army fell upon the aliens.

The battle waged for three days and three nights. Those aliens called upon their spirit power. Lightening and thunder shot from the *sticks* they were carrying and many braves fell dying to the ground. But the others came on.

"The waters of the creek ran red with blood, and the hills echoed the cries of the wounded and dying, but still they fought. In the end the chief of the alien beings and some of his men escaped to the spirit. It swallowed them and moved away. Many braves lay dead from the power of the thunder sticks and even more were wounded.

"But," the shaman concluded, "It was a victory for our ancestors because the aliens and their spirit power never returned."

Oogli had been listening to the narrative with great intensity. In his mind he could see the strange white faced, light-eyed aliens. He could imagine the terror of the villagers who they had visited and had plundered. The battle, itself, with the screams and the blood, and the roar of the magical *thunder sticks*, was as vivid to him as if he had been personally witnessing it.

"I have told you this story as a warning," the old man said, "The aliens and their spirit power have gone for now, but some day they may return. People cannot destroy the spirits, with great courage we may be able to control them, or to prevent them from harming us. We must always be prepared and vigilant. Some day, Oogli, I believe you will be a powerful *siem*. You must be ready to deal with any force, including the spirit beings, should they come again and prey upon the people. Remember my words."

"I will remember," the boy promised.

"And now I have another story to tell you. This happened not so long ago. I know about it because it happened when I was still a strong man, able to hunt and fight. In truth, I am here because of the terrible thing I am about to tell you."

"When your father was a young man, long before you were born, he and the other men of the Lummi people decided to go into the mountains to hunt. At the same time the women and girls, with some elders, came to this island to camp and gather seafood for winter storage.

"It was summertime and the weather was pleasant so the living was comfortable on the island. Besides that, several other groups of people were camping there too, so everyone was enjoying visiting and exchanging gossip as well as working. No one had any thought of danger. In the evening after supper was over, the fires were allowed to die low and the people relaxed, talking quietly or resting.

"Suddenly the air was rent with screams. Fierce Yakultas warriors leaped from behind bushes and attacked the resting women, children, and old people. Those who resisted were killed, others were herded to the waiting ocean-going canoes to be taken to the far north as slaves.

The warriors had destroyed the Lummi canoes before attacking so the people had no way to escape. One woman, with a few others, managed to take a Northern canoe and escape to the mainland. The rest were either slaughtered, or never seen again.

"When your father Sax ump ki, who was chief even then, returned from the mountains he found the few survivors camped on the beach mourning their losses. He was filled with grief for his dead, but more than that he was angry beyond reason. He blamed himself, for he knew of the raids of the fierce Northerners, and as chief he should have made provisions for the defenseless members of his tribe.

"He swore vengeance. And he swore that never again, as long as he was chief, would women and children die at the hands of invaders. He drew apart and nursed his rage and his grief. Then, as now, I was his mentor, so he came to me when at last reason and calm returned to him. Together we explored ways to accomplish his oath.

"The survivors did not blame Sax ump ki directly. Instead they said that it was the absence of the chief that caused the tragedy. They said, 'If he had been there, with his great protective *spirit power*, all would have been well. The Yakultas could never have prevailed against the powers of Sax ump ki.'

"Time went on. The people returned to their village overlooking the pass between the mainland and Lummi Island. Sax ump ki held councils of war, planning and explaining the tactics he would use when the Yakultas returned, as he knew they would. Every warrior knew what he was to do when the invaders came. Lookouts were constantly watching the waters where the canoes would come sweeping through — canoes such as you have not seen, Oogli, mighty, high on the prow — built to carry fifty men through terrible turbulent waters.

"Then one day the call came. The sentinels had spotted war canoes closing in on the village site. Immediately, the plan went into action.

"Women and children ran into the dense forest behind the village to hide. Those warriors who were most adept at battling at sea leaped into their canoes and waited near a point of land which is often submerged to form an island near the village. The other warriors were hidden near the shore ready to ambush the Yakultas.

Just as Sax ump ki expected, when the invaders saw the warriors waiting in their canoes to do battle, they accepted the challenge and set upon them. The Lummi warriors put up a sham resistance and then paddled furiously toward the shore where the main force waited. Then, ramming their canoes onto the beach they made a rush toward the warriors, closely followed by the Yakultas.

"The Northerners were quickly surrounded by the Lummi warriors, and although they fought valiantly for several hours, they had no hope of escape.

"Not one Yakultas survived to take word home about their terrible defeat, and not one Lummi man was lost," the Shaman said.

"Sax ump ki had his revenge and he could hold his head high. He is a great warrior, and his protective magic is so great that he was never touched in battle."

Oogli felt pride in being the son of so great a man. But he felt humble, too. How could he ever expect to follow after a man like his father. His older brother, Cha wentz, he was a warrior already, perhaps he could become as great and as wise and as brave as Sax ump ki — but Oogli?

The shaman seemed to sense the boy's concern. He looked kindly at Oogli. He drew some dried knick knick from a pouch that he carried around his neck and, reaching for his pipe that lay on the ground beside him he carefully tamped the tobacco into the bowl. Then he drew a partly burned twig from the smoldering fire and lit the pipe, drawing deeply.

Oogli sat quietly, sensing that there was more to be said, and that the old shaman was measuring his words before uttering them.

"There are many kinds of men," he said after a long silence. "Some are born to action — to fight, to strive, to make themselves heard. Others are born to think, to feel, to reason. Each is a leader in his own way. My son, the secret of it — the magic of it — is to know which way is your way.

"Do not strive to be that which you are not. If you are to be a warrior and a leader like your father, then be it. Search for the spirit gifts which will make you a great warrior and a wise and true leader of men.

"But if your mind lies in another direction, do not hesitate to take that way. Then you must search for power that will help you to be a leader of men, but one who works through another calling. A great canoe maker is truly a person of value. One, like myself, who can heal and advise is also important. So it is. But whatever path you walk, work with every gift you have to be the best that it is in you to be. That is our way."

Oogli thought about all that the old man had told him. His mind went back to the story about the massacre. It had occurred on the very island where he was sitting. It seemed so real. He thought he could almost hear the screams of the women and children.

"The men were angry, but they must have also felt very sad when they found the dead people and knew that their wives and children had been carried away, and that they would never see them again."

"Sad...yes," the old man agreed. "But more than that. They...we, for I was there, too, we were angry at ourselves. I was chief shaman then...yes, it was me more than any other who was to blame. I could have protected them. I had the power to do it."

"Is that why you stay here?" Oogli wanted to know.

"Yes," Tselique replied. "I stay to guard the graves of those who died and to do penance for my wrong. There is another reason, too. I shall have vengeance if ever again the Northerners return." Hatred showed like a raging fire from the old man's eyes. Oogli cringed, as with pain, from the power that shot from them. In a moment, like a sudden squall at sea, the storm died and the old man was again composed.

"Now it is late," he said, "and you are tired. Lie down in this old house. In the morning I will tell you more."

Oogli did as the shaman told him to, but he could not sleep. His weariness, the storm, the story of the spirit visitors and of the massacre, even Tselique himself, had put his mind on edge. He lay on an old cattail mat on the sleeping platform that ran around three sides of the house. Staring up at the ancient roof he could see stars through openings where the boards had rotted and fallen away. He wondered what it had been like when there were people living here, long before the Northerner's raid. How terrible, he thought, for the old man to be all alone with his memories.

Toward morning Oogli fell into a sleep filled with dreams of children crying, of shamen visiting the dead, and of monsters with white wings rising from the sea. By the time he awoke the sun was beaming through the broken ceiling warming his body. The old shaman was busying himself with a fire on the hearth and Oogli could see that he was simmering some salmon in the cooking box. It smelled good and brought him out of his bed.

"Ha," the old man said. "You smelled the fish. Bathe quickly and then you can eat."

Oogli decided that he liked the old shaman. He was kind, and for the first time in months he could eat all he wanted, and without having to regurgitate. His delighted grin betrayed his feelings.

"I know," the old man said, "you are a boy in training. I am making it too easy for you. But a little lapse won't harm, and to make up for it I have some things to tell you."

Oogli's mouth was filled with the savory salmon chowder. It was impolite to speak while eating, so he kept his eyes properly lowered and continued to enjoy his meal.

"The spirit quest that you are training for is the most important event of your life," the shaman was saying. "It is necessary for you to be ready for it both mentally and physically. You already know that. But do you know that you must also be completely honest about your experiences? Some think they can fool others, pretend to have a vision or that they are training hard. In the end those people will come to witness their own destruction."

Tselique regarded the boy solemnly. For a long time he simply sat on the edge of the sleeping platform and studied Oogli. He seemed to be peering into the inner fiber of this lad who had been sent to him for instruction.

Oogli felt a bit discomfited, but refreshed by his night's sleep and with his stomach satisfied he felt up to anything, even the deep scrutiny that he was undergoing. He felt alert and very much alive and in control of himself. True, his arms ached a little from yesterday's paddling, and his back caused him some pain, but his mind was ready for the challenges that this day would surely bring.

The old man spoke at last, "these are true stories that I am about to tell you. Listen and learn from them."

"I will hear and remember what it is you wish to tell me," Oogli answered in the respectful way that he knew one must use when speaking to a shaman.

The old man nodded, satisfied, his eyes meeting the boy's briefly. In that moment Oogli felt electricity—a sharp sense of magnetism between himself and Tselique. He recalled hearing the elders of his village say, "Be careful. Never look a shaman in the eyes, some can kill or harm with just a look if they have an 'evil eye.'" Oogli rejected that thought as soon as it occurred to him. "He is good. I have no need to fear him," he decided.

"Now," the old man said, "there was a young man who had been in training. When the time came for his spirit quest he said good-bye to his family and taking his canoe he paddled to a far place. He was gone for a long time, so long that he was given up for dead. But one day he returned looking healthy and robust. Indeed he had become a strapping man and he carried himself with authority.

"The people knew that he must have had a powerful vision and undoubtedly possessed a truly great spirit gift, but since it was never revealed exactly what the vision had been, or the true nature of the gift, they could only surmise what it might be.

"It was customary then, just as it is now, for the family of the boy to give a great feast and to invite the entire village and distant people as well to honor him and to recognize his new-found power.

"When the people had gathered, the boy's family gave great gifts to their guests and fed them with a great feast. They did this so that all would know that they were a great family with much wealth, just as your family will do for you, my son, when you receive your gift," Tselique smiled at Oogli.

"Later the drums began to beat and those who possessed spirit power felt it coming upon them and they danced their power and sang their songs. The boy felt his own new power coming upon him and a song began to form in his mind. Almost without his own knowledge he rose and began to dance. The drummers picked up the beat of his song and the people began to sing the words with him. The boy's feet flew around the longhouse stomping and turning until at last he dropped with exhaustion.

"When he had revived he knew that his spirit power was still with him and that it wanted expression. He knew, too, that his people and their guests wished for proof that he actually had a *gift*. So he called some young men to him and said, 'Go to the place that I shall describe to you and bring back what awaits you there.'

"When the men learned where they were to go they pushed their canoes into the water and were soon lost to sight around a point of land. The people waited and some time later the canoes returned loaded with all sorts of seafood. There were crabs and clams and fish of all sorts in such abundance that the canoes were about to swamp.

" 'All of this was waiting for us when we reached the place he directed us to,' the young men said.

" 'He has a great gift,' the delighted villagers agreed. 'Never again will we go hungry.' They honored him.

"Now there was another young man in the village who was lazy and refused to keep training. Everyone feared that he would amount to nothing. He watched the way the people praised the first boy for his gift and he became jealous.

"'I have had a vision too,' he boasted. 'If you will go to the place I will tell you about and bring back what you will find there you will see what a great gift I have received.' So the young men again took to their canoes and went to the place. When they returned the waiting people asked, 'What did you find?' 'This,' one of them replied as he hurled a small spider crab onto the beach.

"Angry, the people turned on the lazy boy. 'You have had no vision and you have no gift. You lied to us. You are a disgrace to your people. You do not deserve to live'.

"They slew him," the shaman said. He paused for a while so that Oogli could consider the meaning of the stories, and then he continued. "It is a serious thing, this quest for the vision that brings a spirit gift. Only a true vision will bring power to you. If you imagine it, or try to pretend, you will be found out and the consequences will be severe. Do not forget the lesson of the false *squedelich*."

Oogli could feel the shaman's eyes boring into him. He was afraid to look at the old man for the power emanating from him seemed to be very strong.

"You fear me," Tselique commented, "do not. You are of my lineage...I want to help you. But you must remember, and it is my duty to remind you, that the spirit you will seek is powerful and not always willing to cooperate. Some spirits may even try to harm you. There is danger, yes, but remember there is also danger from your own people if your gift is not a true one.

"I have spoken. It is time for you to return to your village."

It was with some sadness that Oogli pushed his canoe into the open water. He looked back at the shaman. He seemed so old and thin and alone standing on the beach that the boy hesitated for a moment before he sent his canoe on its way with a strong stroke. "He is of our family, I wish he would come back with me," Oogli thought, but another look at the resolute figure convinced him that Tselique was doing exactly what he wanted to do. "I will see him again," Oogli knew.

His mind was preoccupied with the old shaman and the stories that he had told. Oogli was so absorbed in his thoughts that he scarcely realized that he was paddling. The canoe seemed to guide itself, running effortlessly across the glassy-smooth water. His village grew larger and larger until he could see people gathering on the beach. Compared to the struggle of the outward trip coming home was so easy that the boy marveled. "It could be the power of the shaman," he decided. "Some spirit has been helping me, that much I know."

He could make out his family standing closest to the place where he would beach his canoe. His father stood a little apart from his mother and Latsi. When he was closer his cousins ran out into the water preparing to grasp his bow line and pull him to shore. Soon Latsi was in the water, too, laughing and waving to him.

"This is all for me," Oogli realized with pleasure as he slid his canoe toward the beach.

"It is good that you are back," his father called to him. Latsi ran to the boat while his cousins pulled it high on the beach out of reach of the incoming tide. Oogli could see his mother watching him, smiling. "I wish she would come to me," he thought, yearning for the way she used to speak to him and touch him, "But I'm becoming a man, such things won't do."

"Oogli," his sister tugged at him, "tell us about it. Were you afraid?"

"Afraid?" he laughed. "No..." he started to boast a little, enjoying the attention, but then he remembered the story of the false *squedelich*. "Be truthful," the old shaman had advised him. "Well...maybe I was a little bit afraid when the storm came up," he admitted.

In the longhouse that night Oogli recounted all that had happened, even telling the stories the shaman had told him. The children sat round-eyed, hearing every word. The elders listened too, with great interest, nodding their approval.

When Oogli had finished his recital, his father Sax ump ki, rose to speak. "I perceive that my son has accomplished his mission. The shaman of whom he speaks is my mother's brother. It is he who directed my own period of training. He has honored my son by telling him stories of our family. When the winter ceremonies are upon us Oogli will have a part, for he is now ready."

Autumn came. The vine maples turned red then gold and the leaves fell. The wild geese began their migrations to the south, flying overhead in huge formations, their constant honking filling the air with sound. Ducks, too, sensing the coming winter, were circling, testing their strength before departing.

All of this Oogli noticed as he stood on the beach looking out toward the distant islands. Latsi saw him there when she brought a basket of clam shells from the longhouse to toss on the garbage heap which had become a long, snaking mount just above the beach. Sensing an opportunity to speak to her brother, who had become almost a stranger to her, she approached Oogli.

"My brother," she began, quite formally, "I would speak to you."

"Oh...Latsi" Oogli was startled from his reverie.

"I don't see you any more," she complained. "We used to be friends. Now these past months we are strangers. I don't like it."

"It is the way things are, little sister. It is a hard thing to become a man...I am not a child anymore," then he added ruefully, "But neither am I a man. See the geese? See how they fly, with one strong he-goose at the head of the wedge. Do you know how hard it is to be that one creature?"

"No," Latsi answered. "But he must be very special to be chosen by the others."

51

"He wasn't chosen," Oogli answered, "he earned the right to lead. He is the strongest, the wisest and the bravest of the geese. He must break the wind for the others. See how they fly just behind and to the side? They are in the trough of the wind. And he must lead them to food and resting places all during the time that they are flying to their winter home. All the geese are in his care."

"He must be very wise to find the way," Latsi commented. "That is the place I must take," Oogli said quietly. "Father has spoken of it. I must train hard and learn much to be able. That is why we don't have time together, Latsi. It is hard for me. You must understand that."

"Oh yes, I do," Latsi assured him, "and I know you will be a great chief someday. But I wish I could help you. Isn't there any way I can make it easier?"

"No one can," Oogli replied, "It's not supposed to be easy."

Just then their father emerged from the woods behind the house dragging some poles. "Oogli," he called, "I need some help."

"We will talk again, little sister," he called to Latsi as he ran to Sax ump ki.

"We need to take some deer," Sax ump ki said, "The winter ceremonies will be upon us soon and the feasts we must give will require much food. We will need more than usual this year."

Oogli wondered about the great need for food and felt that somehow the coming events involved him.

"Come, I'll show you how we get deer the easy way."

Oogli stooped to pick up the poles that his father had laid on the ground but Sax ump ki stopped him. "No, I'll carry these, you get the net from my canoe and follow me."

The net, made of twisted inner-cedar bark, was bulky and heavy. It was all that Oogli could do to lift it from the boat but he had long ago learned not to complain. "If

52

one tries hard enough one can do impossible things," he told himself.

Hoisting the net onto his shoulders, he trudged up the beach toward his waiting father. The load did seem to get lighter and Oogli smiled to himself, "I'm getting better at the impossible." He followed Sax ump ki along a path that ran parallel to the beach and out to a point at the southern end of the crescent shaped bay. There the land thrust like an arm out into the sea.

"Here we'll drive the poles into the ground," Sax ump ki announced, "placed about ten feet apart."

Using digging sticks, their points hardened by fire, the pair set the poles into the earth and with stone mauls they drove them down until they were solidly in place.

"Now we will tie the net to the poles," Sax ump ki said.

That done, the man and boy set to work cutting branches to disguise the poles and net.

"Now," Sax ump ki spoke with satisfaction, "we will become herders of deer. You and I will go back into the forest and make a great commotion. If there are deer there we will frighten them and make them run this way—wham! into the net. They will entangled their antlers and perhaps break their necks. Then we will have venison for the women to smoke and dry."

The forest was dark. The sun barely filtered through the treetops so far overhead. There was a dead smell about it, the odor of decaying leaves and wood and many small things. It was a frightening place to be, so different from the openness of the beaches. Oogli lost sight of his father who had moved apart, the better to drive the deer. Somewhere in the distance he heard the eerie scream of a cougar. "The cat is hunting, too," he thought. "I hope he doesn't come for me. Is that the way it is? To hunt and to be hunted?" Suddenly Oogli was repulsed. "I do not want to be a hunter," he said aloud. "My father is a great hunter and he is proud of it. But I do not want that gift. I must be careful not to attract a hunting spirit."

Just then he heard his father's hunting chant, "a ha ya ya...a ha ya ya..." "It is time," Oogli thought and he began to shout and beat a stick on the trees as he pushed his way through the underbrush toward the peninsula and the net. He heard little rustlings as small creatures skittered away.

"A ha ya ya...a ha ya ya" Sax ump ki sang as he beat bushes and whacked his way toward the deadly net.

"Ho ho...ho ho," Oogli shouted. There was a crashing in the forest ahead of him and Oogli knew that a deer or elk had been startled.

On they went, coming up on either side of the point. The deer became visible. It was a big buck racing ahead of them. The moment of impact with the net stunned the deer who fell silently to the ground, his proud neck broken.

"See!" Sax ump ki called, "See how easily it is done?"

"Yes," Oogli answered, staring at the inert form that had been running a moment before. "No," he said to himself. "I do not want to be a hunter."

The Feast

Autumn went quickly. There was much to do to prepare for the winter feasts and the ceremonies that accompanied them.

The people both anticipated and feared that time of the year when the skies grew dark and the north wind blew, bringing icy rains and snow with his chilling breath. That was the time when the spirits returned from their wanderings about the earth. Strange things happened then, supernatural and unexplainable events occurred. Some of the people, those who possessed powerful spirits, became ill with the *spirit sickness* and could only be healed when that presence made itself felt through its own song. Once the spirits had *come out* the power of the people was great and wondrous — fearful things happened.

Everyone in the village had a role to play in the preparations for the feasts that would be given, for the visitors that would arrive, and most of all for the reception of the supernatural beings who would make their presence felt during those cold, wet winter nights.

Some of the women, under the direction of Oogli's grandmother, took stock of the food supplies. It was their responsibility to see that there was plenty to feed several hundred guests for a week or more as well as to see the village through the hard months ahead.

The old woman grumbled as she inspected storage boxes, chiding an unfortunate young woman now and then for improperly smoked clams or salmon or berry cakes already turning moldy. She was a hard mistress, but she knew from experience that a poor food supply meant starvation and suffering for the family.

Oogli's mother, a fine basket maker, organized the other women and girls into a basketry team, mending broken baskets and creating new ones. Many cattail mats were needed too, for diners to sit upon, and there was the inner bark of the cedar tree to be shredded for use as napkins. Cooking mats, tongs with which to handle hot cooking rocks, ladles, water boxes, and watertight cooking baskets all were needed. She had a mountain of domestic tasks to attend to.

The men looked to their ceremonial boxes where all the accouterments for the dances, the initiations, and the dramas were kept. Masks, some so ancient that no one knew when they had been created, were touched up and new ones were created to replace those beyond repair. Dance regalia — costumes reflecting the spirit power of the wolf, bear, eagle, raven to name a few — were examined and repaired. Anklets of deer hooves were inspected for broken pieces and decay. The stench of boiling fresh hooves permeated the air of the longhouse. There was always the need for new rattles to beat out the time when a dancer moved to the cadence of his own spirit dance.

Oogli was given many tasks: to clean out the gelatin from the evil-smelling hooves; drill holes in shells to be strung or carve small wooden paddles to be sewn on dance regalia; grind pigments and mix with salmon eggs for the masks. All of the demands on his time and energy drew from his strength and he became edgy and resentful. But Oogli kept his feelings to himself and whether he realized it or not, he was adding valuable knowledge to a reservoir that someday would be of value to him.

One evening, in the midst of all the industry, Oogli's grandfather rose from his place at the head of the long-house, rapped the wooden platform with his talking stick, waited for silence, and began to speak.

"My people," he said in the dignified tone he assumed when he had something important to say, "it has come to my mind that it is time for us to give a great feast. Our women have laid in much food, our village is prosperous, we have many possessions, more than we need for our own use."

The family seemed to gasp all together in one breath. Such an announcement, coming so late in the year meant much work to be done in a short time. Beyond that, it meant that an important event was about to take place. They wondered what it was that the old *siem* had in mind — a potlatch, to be sure, but for what purpose?

Oogli, the boy in training, was particularly shaken by the thought of a feast at his house. "Somehow," he thought, "it will involve me." He had heard tales of tests of endurance that other boys had undergone during the winter ceremonies, terrible tests involving great pain which must be borne in silence. "Oh no!" he cried inwardly, "Not that!"

His grandfather was looking at him, but Oogli could not meet his gaze. "This boy we call Oogli," the old man said, "it is time he had a true name, one that he can carry with pride. He has proven himself to be worthy many times. I have thought about it, and a name has come to me. It is a name that he should have."

"A naming!" Oogli almost shouted, but instead he kept his eyes properly lowered, and sat quietly, humbly. "I am to receive my real name."

Oogli observed it all, for although the activity and concern centered about the need for a name to be properly bestowed upon him, he himself was not involved. In fact, as Oogli quickly learned much to his delight, the entire household was so caught up in the immense task before them that his rigidly controlled training was largely forgotten. He was able to roam freely, to be his own person for the first time in what seemed to him to have been an eternity.

The elders were talking seriously, grouped together in Grandfather Sta nek's quarters at the far end of the great house. Oogli eased up close so that he could hear their conversation.

"The name I have chosen is Cha it zit," the old man was saying. "It is a worthy name. It belonged to my great-uncle who carried it proudly. Before that it was owned by an ancestor who had a great experience with a raven. The name carries power."

"True," answered another who Oogli knew to be a shaman. "But it is not in your power alone to bestow the name. You must get the approval of all of his descendants. They, too, have a right to say who receives such a great name."

"Yes...yes...I know," the old man answered. "I plan to leave tomorrow to visit my relatives and to ask for their consent and invite them to the naming feast as well."

"It is well," one after another, the elders gave their approval. "Who will you take?" an old man, who sat hunched under a mountain goat blanket asked.

"I will take Cha wentz, Oogli's half brother, and Sax ump ki, his father. My relatives will welcome them and will have difficulty denying such a strong appeal for the name."

A group of women sat in a circle around a cooking fire that had burned to embers. Oogli turned his attention to them. He heard his mother say, "It is important that everything goes just right. Any slip, any mistake could be disastrous for Oogli. He will be very vulnerable while he is waiting for the name he is to receive. Once it is spoken the power of the name will be unrestrained. It could do damage. We must all be very careful not to offend any former owner of the name, those in the villages of the dead are to be guarded against."

"Namings have always frightened me," Oogli recognized the voice of his father's brother's wife.

"What frightens me," said another of the women, "is all the gifts we must give. There is so little time to make them. The honored guests will expect blankets."

"Yes," Wanana agreed, "The men decide these things, but they don't think about the difficulties we must face. How many blankets suitable for giving do we already have?"

Oogli crept away. He could not concern himself with the affairs of the women.

The sound of an adz cutting into wood caught his attention. "Someone is working, even at night," he thought. "It must be important, whatever he is doing." Creeping along the outer shadows of the house, away from the flickering fires, he spotted the carver of cedar bending over a length of wood.

"You are working late," Oogli observed as he crouched beside the artisan.

"It is to be a mask for the squai quai dance," the carver answered. "You are keeping all of us busy, Oogli."

"Yes, I know," the boy replied a bit wistfully. "Every one is busy but me. I think I even miss not running errands and all the work I had to do. At least then people were noticing me."

Oogli watched as the carver deftly shaped the mask. Huge bulbous eyes protruded from a large flat face. Between them, where the nose should have been, a form had been roughly carved to resemble the head of a bird. Where

an ordinary mask might have had upright ears this squai
quai mask possessed two animal heads. The mouth was
small and weak and had been cut through so that one could
look out of it. There was much yet to be done before the

black and red paint could be applied in the manner that only that carver could use, Oogli knew, but already the mask seemed to possess a reality of its own. As he watched, visions of the dance of these masks came to mind — an exciting dance it was, with inner meaning but comedy as well. Soon, he realized with a feeling of wonderment, the dance would be performed for his benefit.

"For me," he said, "you are carving this special mask for me. When the dance is performed, it will be for me."

Oogli wandered off, seeking a dark, quiet place in which to realize, for the first time, the incredibility of it all. Even during the hardest part of his training, he had not stopped to think of the utter dedication that his entire family had felt to his eventual success as an important member of the group and an eventual leader. Now the full impact of giving a proper feast became clear to Oogli. He understood the meaning of the labor involved, the prestige laid bare to ridicule if all did not go well, the cost in worldly goods, the risk of the family's survival if there was not enough food to give both a feast and still feed themselves for the winter.

He found his place in a far corner of the longhouse behind some storage boxes. There he curled up, wrapped in his bearskin robe. Standing, as he was between the carefree days of his youth and the burdens and expectations of adulthood, his mind vacillated between the way it had been, and never would be again, and the way it might be, if all went well.

He thought about his mother's gentle touch and her soft voice. He missed that with an ache that he would not permit himself to recognize. Since his training had begun there had not been any outward communication between them, only a look, a gesture or a feeling. He knew it was not considered seemly for a boy at the edge of manhood to consort with women. His own mother — she who had been of such importance in his life — had slipped back as custom demanded to let him become a man. Oogli wondered what sacrifice she was making, of how her soul might suffer, but he knew she was doing the necessary thing, and because of that she would hold her head high and bear herself with pride. "It is important that I do the same," he told himself.

In a rush of feeling Oogli remembered the first bow that he had owned. It had been given to him by his grandfather on an occasion that he would never forget. In his mind he could see Sta nek standing before him, the toy bow in his hand. "You may be a great hunter someday like your father," the old man had said, "or a warrior such as Cha wentz may become...but you are different. I see a future greatness in you, greatness that is of the heart, not of the bow. Take this small gift from me, join the other boys, practice with it, grow proficient in its use, but do not make it your life."

Oogli recalled running freely with the other boys, playing the games they played. He shot his bow and hit the mark more often than he missed it. But it had not been as important to him to excel as it was to his companions. He remembered swimming in the bay, the cold water tingling his naked body. More fish than boy he seemed to be in those days. His memory wandered back to the times when he first learned to paddle a canoe, to snare small animals, to catch fish, to start a fire.

Suddenly he realized, lying in his dark place, that all of the experiences he lived through in the past were leading up to the events soon to come. Each day of his childhood had been a learning time. "No," he revised his thinking, "each day I have been led to know the skills I will need to take my place when I am a man." Even the evenings, when the family sat together around the hearth fire and the elders told stories of long ago, he now knew had been teaching sessions. It was important that he know the tribal traditions and his heritage, for someday, he now understood, he must pass it on to others.

As he lay snug under his robe many things that he had rebelled against or puzzled over began to come clear to Oogli. For the first time he saw his place in the tribal scheme.

"And now," he thought to himself, "now it is all coming together. I am to receive a great name, one to help me become all that it is in me to be. Am I worthy of such an honor?"

The tremendous question lay upon him like a mountain, seeming to suffocate him with self-doubt. It was in that state of mental anguish that Oogli eventually drifted off to sleep — a sleep in which a great boulder sat upon his chest.

The next morning the delegation, headed by Sta nek, left for villages a day's run by canoe from their own community of Swetquem. Eleq, situated a short distance up the great Neutsack River, and Kwakas, farther up just short of a great log jam, would be visited first. Then down a fork of that river to Momli which lay above the beach on the surging waters of the strait down which the northern raiders came, was Temxwigqsan, located on a point of land facing to the south where the bay and the straits ran together. From there it was but a short trip back to Swetquem. The group would be gone for a number of days, for at each village they would be properly received and honored with a feast. Then a lengthy discussion would ensue before permission could be given to use the name that had been chosen for Oogli. The whole procedure must be done properly, with all the customary rituals observed, if the name was to be approved and if it was to rest easily on Oogli.

Watching from the beach, flanked by his own family, the boy saw his grandfather being carried to the finest canoe on the back of his personal slave. Oogli knew that as

64

a man of high rank, it would have been unseemly for Sta nek to wade to his canoe when he had a strong slave to carry him. Then the slave returned for Sax ump ki, and finally he bore Cha wentz and deposited him in the center of the stout craft. That done, he and a second slave jumped in, one fore and one aft, picked up paddles and prepared to shove off.

"We will return with a great name," Oogli heard his grandfather call confidently. "Let us go," he ordered the slaves.

The people called out encouragement while the canoe shot out into the waters of the bay. Soon it was out of sight.

And so the days passed rapidly, each full of activity. The ambassadors returned with the news that the name had been approved—a name which only a select few knew, a name which must not be spoken aloud until it was presented with the proper ceremony and respect. Messengers were sent to relatives in the nearby villages inviting them to a potlatch in a month's time. The longhouse was cleaned and refurbished. Blankets, baskets, carved trays and boxes were made and piled on the platform occupied by Sta nek.

So that the expected guests would be impressed as well as fed and cared for, huge feast trays were carved for the occasion. Cattail eating mats were woven and cedar bark was shredded to be used as napkins. The storage boxes and baskets bulged with food. Dance regalia—masks, headdresses, and costumes—had been repaired and refurbished. Drums with new skin heads waited to be used. Each new day brought more tasks and challenges. The time grew short and tempers flared with the pressing needs.

Oogli found tension mounting inside of him. What would his real name bring to him? Would he change once he carried it? He wasn't sure he even wanted a "great" name. Would he be able to do it credit? As the time approached he became fidgety and irritable. At night he lay for hours on his sleeping mat, staring at the rafters of the house. All around him he could hear the heavy breathing and snores of sleepers, but no sleep came to him.

The great day came. It was cold and dreary. Rain pelted on the shake roofboards of the longhouse. Occasionally a drop fell through the smoke hole and hissed as it evaporated on the fire below.

All was ready. Gifts were piled high on Sta nek's platform at the far end of the house. The old man, who had given up his living space to accommodate the pile of blankets, hunting and fishing gear, boxes, and baskets, sat on a bentwood box amid the array. He was gloriously clad in a new buckskin shirt, matching leg coverings and apron. Carved miniature paddles placed in rows across the front of his shirt made pleasant clicking sounds as he moved. He wore a necklace of bear claws and on his head was a circlet of woven cedar bark. His talking stick rested nearby, ready for the moment guests should enter.

The women and girls of the family, festive in leather dresses adorned with shells, waited nervously by the low entrance to the house while drummers sat nearby on the edge of the platform, their drums tightened by heat, prepared for the moment when they would be needed.

Oogli observed it all from his place of confinement back in the shadows, partly shielded by cattail mats. He was dressed simply in an apron of the finest mountain goat wool which his mother had woven for this occasion. His hair had been carefully combed and was held in place by a ring of woven inner cedar bark. He had passed the point of nervous apprehension and had become mentally numb. Whatever would be would be, he felt. This curious sense of detachment was a welcome change from his previous state of nerves. For the first time in days he found himself able to observe the activity around him objectively. It was as though he had separated himself from it as a disinterested spectator, watching an event that didn't concern him from a distant mountain top. He delighted in his new mental state and watched the preparations with casual interest.

Latsi, who was standing beside Wanana, looked almost like a woman, Oogli thought. She was dressed in a new gown, one that she had made with their grandmother's help, especially for the occasion. Her hair, caught in two braids and held with a ribbon of fur, was lustrous in its newly-washed blackness.

"My sister is growing up," he observed, "I've been so deep into my own affairs that I haven't noticed. Soon she will be secluded. I must give some time to her while she is still a child. I do not want to lose Latsi," he mused thinking of the distance between himself and his mother. His thoughts carried him to the inevitable time when she would be gone. "After her period of seclusion—when no one can see her except an old woman or two—she will be married and leave this house," his inner voice was saying. "But now all she is thinking of is making this day a great day for me."

As if Latsi caught Oogli's thoughts, she turned, searching for a glimpse of him. He moved his hand, ever so slightly out of the shadows. She saw it, nodded to him, a quiet smile on her face, and turned back to the women.

Outside, a voice called excitedly, "They are coming! They are coming!" Then a young man, a warrior who had been assigned to watch, bounded through the entrance way. "There are three canoes just rounding the point...from Temxwigqsan I think."

Old Sta nek rose from his seat and addressed the waiting people. "Our young men who are already on the beach will greet them. My son, our chief, Sax ump ki, with Cha wentz and others of high rank will escort them to this house. You know what to do when they get here."

The women and girls, looking tense, lined up facing the entrance, while the drummers took their places behind them. Others, both men and women who were to sing, arranged themselves in a semi-circle to one side. All waited quietly.

Suddenly the first guests were at the doorway. The drummers began, softly, and the women, arms outstretched in a friendly gesture moved forward to the slow, dignified motion of the welcoming dance. The singers, taking their cue began the words, following the beat of the drums.

"Hae a luckh ath la ti a
ha haha ha
ha ya ha"

The simple words, which were repeated over and over again with variations in intonation and rhythm, meaning "We are happy you are here," filled the longhouse with a pleasant sound, and they filled Oogli with humility.

"It is beginning," he realized, not excited but still calm under the influence of the strange detached mood which had settled upon him. He saw his grandfather rise, rap his talking stick on the plank platform with a resounding tattoo and then wait until all eyes were upon him.

"You have honored my house by coming. You are welcome here. Come and sit at our fires, eat of our food and rest from your journey."

From his place, partly hidden by the hanging mats, Oogli watched the guests as they arrived. Many of the faces were familiar — people from villages he had visited with his family during other winters. One face in particular caught his eye. It was not an unusual face, he admitted, but it had a quality that drew his interest. The girl it belonged to was about his age, maybe a bit younger, he conceded. There was an air of mischief about her — the way her eyes seemed to smile as if at some secret joke and the way she tilted her head — like a curious puppy would have. He noticed, too, that she carried herself proudly, not with bowed head and downcast eyes the way most of the village girls did. Oogli saw that her dress was rich, a fringed, white buckskin gown, hung with olive shells. When she was lost from view, moving out of the line of his vision, he wondered who she was, what village she belonged to, surely it was none of those he was familiar with.

Then he caught himself. "Girls," Oogli muttered to himself. He had no time for girls and their foolishness. Still the vision of her face stayed in his mind.

The longhouse was now filled with guests. They stood politely, waiting. Some time passed before Sta nek rapped his talking stick. He spoke, "Again I say to you welcome. You have honored this house and this village by your presence. I will now seat you."

One by one he called the names of the guests, the most important ones first. These braves were escorted to their places, those to be honored were placed closest to the old man on his platform. Others, of lesser rank, were ranged about the large room, with the poorest being given places by the entrance way.

Again, Sta nek rapped his stick. "I call upon those who will witness this potlatch," he said. Four men, elders all, rose from their places and stood for all to see.

"These men, from the Samish people, from the Semiahmoo people, from the Swinomish people, and from our sister village of Momli have come from a distance at my request. They have agreed to tell all of their people about this event. If it is a great potlatch (and I truly say it will be), they will acclaim it. But if it is not great, they will say so, for in these affairs all must be honestly done.

"Now, my guests, you must be hungry. Let the feasting begin!"

The women, all part of Oogli's family — aunts, cousins, his mother and grandmother and sister — spread new cattail mats on the clean-swept dirt floor. When that was done, they invited the guests to sit. Next, wooden buckets of water and ladles were passed among them so all might drink and cleanse their mouth — the better to enjoy the food to come. Girls appeared carrying baskets filled with shredded cedar bark to be used as napkins.

Then great trays of steaming food were carried in from the fires of a neighboring house. There were chunks of dried salmon that had been gently simmered to soften it, with side dishes of fish oil in which to dip it. A chowder of clams, seasoned and thickened with seaweed, appeared. There were cakes of sun-dried berries and venison jerky to add variety to the meal.

The people ate quietly, their eyes lowered, enjoying each morsel as they helped themselves from the communal trays. Ladles were used for the soup, fingers for the solid food.

Oogli noticed that his grandfather did not partake of the food. He sat on his carved bench leaning on the talking stick, watching the gathering intently.

"He is uneasy," Oogli thought. He had not been allowed to join the group, but Latsi had brought some dried salmon which he tore with his teeth and tried to swallow. His stomach resented the hard half-chewed food and let him know. That, together with a feeling of anxiety which had begun to build in him, displacing his earlier euphoria, brought on nausea. "I'm going to be sick," he moaned inwardly. "But I can't be sick. What will be said about me? 'A boy is to be named, but he is not worthy of a great name…it makes him sick, the name is too powerful for his body.' I will not be sick!"

Oogli was so intent upon dominating his protesting stomach that he mentally blocked out the activity in the longhouse. Suddenly he was jerked back to reality by the sound of his grandfather's talking stick banging on the wood platform.

"I have seen that you enjoyed the food we prepared for you," he was saying. "Now, while the women are clearing away the remains of the feast, I will ask Tselique, my brother, who you all know as a shaman possessing great powers, to speak to you of the reason why we are gathered here together. It is a great occasion for my family, one which you will share with us."

Oogli was surprised to see the old man whom he had met on the small island appear from behind the screen which stood behind his grandfather. He was dressed in a black bear robe, with only a buckskin loin cloth underneath. A necklace of bear claws hung around his neck, and he wore a crown of bear claws on his head. His grey hair was matted, and his total appearance was frightening.

"He looks different," Oogli thought, "scary, even, not like the kind person who fed me and told me about my ancestors."

The old shaman walked unsteadily to the front of the platform, using his stick to balance himself. He stood there, peering at the people with an intensity that made them squirm and appear to be most uneasy.

"They say shamen have an evil eye and can kill a man with a look," Oogli recalled. "I'm glad he's not looking at me like that. I wonder what he is going to do?"

After a period of strained silence, the old man raised his hand. Then he spoke.

"You have been called to witness the naming of a boy who is soon to become a man," he said in a throaty, husky voice. "This boy has been in training, directed by his father Sax ump ki who you all know as a great chief and leader of men. This boy, too, may someday be headman of this village. He has a powerful lineage. His father, my nephew, is of the Lummi people. His mother, Wanana, is of the Samish, of the nobility. This boy's house and family is one to be respected, as you who are here all know."

A murmur of agreement arose among the guests, and grew to a crescendo. Tselique waited until the voices had become silent. Then he rapped his stick sharply and called out, "I ask the boy we have known as Oogli to come out here."

Oogli's rebellious stomach seemed to turn completely over. He caught his breath—felt his knees begin to buckle under him—and mechanically began to move forward. Not quite knowing how he accomplished it, Oogli emerged from the shadows that had concealed him and walked across the platform to where his grandfather and Tselique stood.

"Here stands the boy who had earned the right to a man's name," the shaman said. "I ask you all to acknowledge that this is true, that the one we call Oogli is worthy."

Voices echoed from around the room. A man's voice rang out, "I know that he is worthy." Then other voices were heard to say, "Yes, he is worthy."

Oogli heard and felt his body gaining strength. His stomach no longer gave him trouble, and his legs felt strong. The spirit of the occasion was making itself felt in him. He was inwardly pleased that the men in the gathering respected him, but he also realized that the respect was directed toward his family, rather than himself. Standing so close to Tselique, Oogli seemed to feel the power that he radiated. He dared not look into the old shaman's eyes, so the boy kept his head lowered, just to be safe.

Tselique seemed to sense Oogli's fear and he said softly so no one else could hear, "Do not fear me, think of me as a friend. Lift up your head. You must be proud this day, for this is the greatest day of your life, so long as you have lived it."

Then he spoke again to the people. "You have approved of this boy. Witnesses, you have heard."

Turning to Oogli and looking directly in his eyes, Tselique said in a loud voice, "I now give you the name of Cha it zit. From this day you will no longer be called Oogli, a child's name, but you will be Cha it zit. Cha it zit. Cha it zit."

The four witnesses stood. One at a time they repeated. "I have witnessed it. His name is Cha it zit.

"Cha it zit," repeated the assembly three times.

Then Sta nek rapped the floor with his talking stick. "It is done." He took a blanket from the pile on his platform and laid it upon the boy's shoulders.

As Oogli, now to be known as Cha it zit, felt the weight of the blanket it was as if some spirit entered into him. He felt more alive than he ever had before. It seemed to him that a great buoyancy was lifting him, carrying him to heights he had never dreamed were possible. He felt that he dominated the scene before him, that this power coming upon him brought with it overwhelming, magnificent strength. He saw himself in a new way and it pleased him. He stood tall as he faced the people.

His father rose from the place he had been sitting near Sta nek and approached Cha it zit. He laid his hands on the boy's shoulders and, looking him directly in the eyes, repeated the name, "Cha it zit…Cha it zit…Cha it zit." There was pride in his voice.

Then followed the prominent men in attendance, each repeating the name three times. Others of lesser importance followed, and then came the women, led by Cha it zit's mother.

"Mother," he pleaded mentally, "acknowledge me, your son, we have become so distant." He saw the love and pride in her eyes, but she only did as the others, saying, "Cha it zit…Cha it zit…Cha it zit."

Then came Latsi. Her eyes were brimming with tears. She took his hand in hers and declared in a firm voice, "Cha it zit...Cha it zit...Cha it zit." The way she said the name brought with it a message from her heart and Cha it zit felt the deep meaning. "We will always be brother and sister. No matter how we may change, that never will," he vowed in his mind.

Suddenly the girl he had noticed earlier stood in front of him. She was so close he could easily have touched her. Cha it zit felt an insane desire to place his hand upon the smooth skin of her face. He did not understand the strange emotion that he felt and did his best to suppress it. She looked at him with eyes so large and shining that he seemed to be drawn into their depths. All of his pride and feeling of importance simply vanished. He felt instead a great sense of inadequacy. How could he even speak to such a superior person as this girl was.

"Cha it zit...Cha it zit...Cha it zit" she said softly and passed by him.

When the last, least guest had returned to his place, Sta nek rapped with his talking stick. "To honor Cha it zit on this great occasion, we, his family, have gifts to distribute. These gifts will remind you of this day and will forever seal the name of Cha it zit."

The women of the family came forward, and as the old man indicated, they carried blankets, trays, baskets, paddles, and all manner of useful and beautiful items to those who were to receive them. Cha it zit watched as his family's wealth and cherished possessions were given away. Soon the great house would be bare. They would be in poverty but the family pride would swell and all would respect them for their great, generous potlatch. The boy took comfort in the fact that as time went by those who had received gifts would be obligated to return gifts of even greater value.

"You have seen that we are a great people," Sta nek concluded the gift giving ceremony. "The hour is growing late, and you must be getting hungry. You will honor us by eating again of our food. We have much, eat till your bellies will hold no more."

Cha it zit heard the invitation with gratitude. He realized that he was exceedingly hungry. In spite of his long periods of semistarvation, of learning to ignore his body's demand for nourishment until he no longer felt the need, even the desire, for food, he was suddenly ravenous. How long had it been since he had eaten, really eaten? He could not remember. All he knew was that his belly ached and that he longed to fill it. The awful thought came, would he be allowed to eat? And if he could put food in his demanding stomach would he then be required to regurgitate it as he had been so many times in the past? Now that he had the status of a great name would his period of training be over?

This thought, that his ordeal might be over, challenged the boy's imagination and brought with it the happy prospect of release. His mind could hardly grasp the thought. Everything else was blotted out, the reality of the moment, the honor he had been given, the girl he had seen, the people assembled before him. He could only grasp the one wonderful idea—the end of his training might have come.

The scene before him blurred and then the faces began to slowly spin. The room was revolving, faster and faster it turned. He felt his body relaxing, crumpling in slow motion. The earthen floor felt good, so good. Cha it zit lay motionless, engulfed in a moving sea of mist and color. Objects rotated slowly around him; canoes, blankets, drums, storage boxes, strange faces he could not identify floated by.

From somewhere far away a voice was saying, "He has had an encounter with a spirit. It is a good sign. He will have great power. The name is strong, already the spirit forces are testing him."

Cha it zit became aware of Tselique and his father standing over him. His mind was awakening but his body was not yet willing to respond.

"We must not disturb him," the old shaman continued. If we arouse him while his soul is away from his body he may die. I will watch him and help him back if his soul becomes lost and cannot return."

"Watch him carefully. Use all of your power, if you must. He must live," Sax ump ki said as he turned to leave.

Cha it zit struggled back to consciousness. When he opened his eyes he saw the old shaman squatting at his side.

"Ha," Tselique grunted, "You have returned of your own will. I thought I might have to come after your soul. But you are strong and have power, that I can see. Now rest. I will get you some food to fill your body."

The hot chowder, rich and nourishing, which Tselique offered Cha it zit warmed his body and brought strength with each spoonful. The old man sat beside the boy as he ate. He didn't speak, but studied Cha it zit's face and seemed to be deep in contemplation.

"I feel better now," Cha it zit said at last.

Without speaking, Tselique took a small bone figure from a leather pouch, which he wore tied around his waist on a leather thong. Cha it zit saw that it was a carving of a raven, simply done.

"This will protect you," the old man said as he pressed it into the boy's hand. "Powerful spirits are waiting to help or harm you. If you can handle them, if you are strong enough, you can become powerful yourself. This amulet, which has aided me many times, possesses magic to help you, too. Keep it always with you."

Cha it zit clutched the carving in his fist. It felt warm and smooth. As he held it, it seemed to him that it became warmer, almost as if it was alive. Was it his imagination or did the figure move in his hand?

The shaman watched him closely. Cha it zit began to feel uneasy. He avoided meeting the old man's eyes. Even though Tselique had asked him not to be afraid, the boy could not bring himself to meet the piercing look that men said could bring death to the unwary.

"Do you feel the spirit of the bone?" Tselique asked him.

"It is warm and feels alive in my hand," Cha it zit answered.

"That is good," the shaman nodded. "You are receptive. What did you feel when your soul left you?"

"It was strange. I saw many things, people I did not know, men with pale, ghostly faces, objects of wealth like canoes, blankets, many things. They floated all around me. It was like I was in a fog—hazy and full of color."

"Do not tell anyone of this," Tselique cautioned. "This may have been a vision—that which you have been preparing for. I do not know what it means, but I do know that if you speak of it you will lose the power it may be bringing to you."

"How will I know if it is really a spirit vision—a true vision?"

"It will come again. If it does not, you must go out and seek it. Come now, we must return to our guests." At the far end of the house by the low entry way men were warming their drums near a fire of glowing coals. They knew that only a tight drum gives out a resonant tone. Others were unwrapping bundles of painted sticks, equipment for playing sla hal. No gathering was complete unless the Salish gambling game of sla hal was part of the activities.

Cha it zit observed the preparations with interest. He had watched adults play the exciting game, their movements tied to the beat of the drum and the sing-song repetition of the sla hal song. He had seen wealth won and lost on the guess for a "bone," but the game had held little interest for him. Like all boys he would rather run and play children's games like tossing a ball, playing tug of war, or shooting his bow, competing with the other boys for arrows. But, for some reason, sla hal intrigued him now.

He knew that he couldn't play the game. He had nothing to wager. Even if he did, no one would accept him as a player for he had not yet proved himself, he was not yet a man. "Anyway," he thought, "I have no skill." A good sla hal player had to be skillful to fool the other team when he hid the bones and he had to be able to guess which hand they were in, male and female bone, when it was his turn to choose. The men had spread a blanket on the floor. On it they laid four cylinders of bone, two plain and two with bands of black. They had placed a board at each side of the blanket—two boards opposite each other. Before the boards eleven tally sticks had been placed, sharpened points in the ground. All was ready. The game would start when Sta nek permitted. Cha it zit vowed that he would be there watching. It became important to learn all he could about sla hal so that when he was permitted to play he would be a winner. "I shall be a great player. All men will respect me," he promised himself.

At the other end of the longhouse Cha it zit saw his father and grandfather talking earnestly. When they noticed him they beckoned him to them. On his way he passed his mother who was supervising the clearing away of the last of the food trays.

"My son," she spoke to him.

"Mother...you addressed me," he whispered.

"Shush," she admonished him, "it is not right for us to be close, now that you are nearing manhood, but I must tell you that I am proud of you this day. I know, too, that your soul left us for a while. I hope all is well with you."

"All is well," Cha it zit assured her.

He passed her by and neared the platform.

"Ah, Cha it zit, you will sit here by me," Sta nek greeted him. "All that is done is in your honor and to give you prestige among the villages."

There was a sharp, staccato drum beat. The guests quickly scrambled onto the raised platforms, leaving the floor space open. Singers gathered in front and to the left of

Sta nek's seat and took up the squai quai song. A dancer,
wearing a squai quai mask, leaped from behind the screen
at the rear of Sta nek's platform and began to do a curious
dance. In a side-stepping, crab-like movement he danced
down the length of the house, always keeping his face
toward the audience, never once turning to either side.
Then he danced backward, still using the special squai quai
step, never turning, never looking behind him until he
reached the place he had entered. He mounted the platform dancing and leaping backwards, and disappeared
behind the screen.

The drums and singers continued. Moments later he again appeared, this time followed by a second dancer who repeated all the motions of the first, moving on down the floor never turning. Suddenly a third dancer appeared, a small fellow, wearing a mask that was a miniature version of the first two. He carried a cedar branch switch in his hand.

Down the house he danced, mimicking the motions of the others. Dancing behind them, he switched them in an effort to distract them and spoil their rhythm. The people watching laughed, while the dancers tried to ignore him.

When they had completed the dance, the original two retired behind the screen. The *clown* danced his way to where Cha it zit was sitting and proceeded to lash him with the whip. The drums picked up in tempo — boom, boom, boom. The singers raised their voices. The sound, the drums pulsating louder and louder, echoed in Cha it zit's consciousness. The booming became a continuous thunder, accented by the lightening of the voices. The lash cut through it all like a knife.

Cha it zit sat as if he were frozen. He made no sound. And then it was over. The dancer leaped behind the screen and was gone. The drums stopped and the great room was silent.

Sta nek stood and tapped the platform deck. "My grandson Cha it zit is now cleansed. He is ready to take his place among us. I ask that you accept him."

There was a murmur of approval. Then the first of the witnesses stood up. "I come to you from the Samish people.

"We have long been friends and allies of the Lummis. I will tell those of our villages of this great occasion. I will tell them that Cha it zit, the grandson of Sta nek and the son of Sax ump ki and of my niece, Wanana, has proven his worthiness to bear the great name."

When he had finished speaking Wanana brought him a string of wampum, rare shells which had been filed to rounds and strung upon a fine nettle twine.

Then the second witness rose and began to speak, "I am from the villages of the Semiahmoos. When I return, all will know of the greatness of this house and of the boy, soon to be a man, the one we now know as Cha it zit. I will speak, too of the fine potlatch that has been given by Sta nek and his family. We, too, have long been friendly to the people of Lummi. Although we are constantly besieged by the Northerners, we stand ready to aid you, should you need us." He, too, received wampum and retired to his place.

The third witness spoke these words, "I come from the Swinomish villages which lie some distance away, south of the Samish people. It is because of our great respect for the Lummi people that we have come. I shall speak highly of this occasion to all I see. Your gifts have been generous, your women hospitable, and your braves courteous. I see the boy Cha it zit has the qualities to become a leader and to follow the example set before him by his elders. I will speak the name Cha it zit with pride, knowing that we two peoples will always be friendly and that when Cha it zit has assumed his place he will feel our influence, and we will feel his."

After he had received his gift, the fourth witness arose. "I am representing the people of Momli. We have seen the boy, Cha it zit since his cradle-board days. We have watched him grow to become the fine boy he is. We will long remember this day when he received his *great name*. We will announce that name to all of our own people and to those of Eleq, Kwakas, and Temxwigqsan, telling of the great occasion we have just witnessed."

He, too, received a wampum string. Wanana retired to stand behind her husband. Again, Sta nek rapped for attention.

"It is done. I and my family invite you to stay with us for as long as you wish. Our food is abundant and our house is open to you. The spirits are returning, some of you have felt them already, and they will wish to enter into the dances which we will do when they make their presence felt. The players of sla hal have already made preparations for the game. Our braves have arranged for games to be played. There will be much to do. But now you are tired. I will leave you to rest, and to do that which pleases you."

The people rose from their places. Some drifted into groups to talk, some left the longhouse to see to their canoes or possessions left outside. Others found a quiet place, wrapped themselves in a blanket and slept.

Cha it zit, exhausted, sought a dark corner in which to revive himself. He needed solitude. He found it behind the cattail mat that had secluded him before the ceremony had begun. There he laid himself down and slipped into a state of semi-consciousness which gradually deepened to sleep.

When he awoke it was dark in the house, except where a single hearth fire glowed. It cast shadows of orange and purple on the outer reaches of its light. He could hear the clacking of sticks beating on boards and the steady singsong of the sla hal song:

"A ha haha
a ya ya ha ya a
a a yaaa
a ha ha ya a
ah y aaa ah."

Over and over the words were repeated, building an intense, almost hypnotic, spell.

"Sla hal!" he said aloud. He surprised himself. The game had never interested him much, but now the sound of the song, the rhythm of the beat gripped him with an intensity that could not be denied. He sat up so that he could see the players.

By the dim glow of the fire he could follow their gestures, pointing, changing hands, swaying, taking counting sticks, all to the cadence of the beating sticks. "I must watch more closely," he decided.

He crept out of his corner and found a place where he could observe the play without being seen. Cha it zit knew the basic rules of the game, about the cylinders of bone, white for male, black banded for female, which the players must guess for, the counters which kept score. He knew, too, that fortunes were bet on the guess for a male bone. A man could be made wealthy or pauperized in a game of sla hal.

He watched the motions of the two players, who sat opposite each other, the blanket between them piled with items of value, flanked by their teams of singers and beaters. They were quick and skillful, performing with the utmost concentration, their faces expressionless. Nothing was said, it was all timed motion, tied to the clacking of the sticks. Cha it zit was completely immersed. The hours passed but he was unaware of the time.

It was Latsi who found him and gently took him by the hand, leading him toward his sleeping place. He followed, completely bemused, his mind echoing the relentless beating of the sticks.

"It is late, brother," she told him. "The game will go on all night, maybe for several days, you must sleep. I fear you will become ill if you don't eat and rest."

"So much has happened to me...I mean inside of me.... I don't understand it," he told her. "Strange things are going on, Latsi, what is taking place in my mind?"

He tumbled into his bed of cattail mats and pulled the mountain goat's wool blanket over his head. A sleep born of exhaustion came upon him and Cha it zit was carried into a dark, dreamless void.

It was late in the morning when the people began to stir. Guests lay everywhere, wrapped in their blankets. One by one they arose and went to the cold salt water to bathe. Women poked in the ashes of the cooking fires, breathing on them and adding tinder to coax a blaze. Breakfast preparations began. Oblivious, the sla hal players continued their game.

All through the night Cha it zit had clutched the amulet given to him by Tselique. Now he turned his thoughts to keeping it safely hidden. A gift such as that, ripe with power, must be cherished and preserved. He looked about for Latsi.

He found her on the path leading to the stream that provided the village with water. She carried a wood bucket to be filled.

"Sister," he called.

She whirled about, a smile on her face. "Are you feeling rested, brother?"

"Yes, thanks to you. I have a favor to ask of you. Could you make me a small buckskin bag with a cord so I could tie it around my neck?"

"I'll ask mother for some scraps," she answered. "I can use her needle to sew with, too. Is this a secret thing you ask?"

"Yes," Cha it zit said.

The day passed quickly. The children played games on the beach, running and chasing each other, falling and getting up to run again. Those who were older organized a competition between the youths of the villages, playing tug of war, using long poles to pull with. The girls called out encouragement while the boys of their village tried to impress them and prove their strength. Tired of that, the girls challenged the boys. When their chores were finished

the women organized the sme tali game, which they played with four beaver teeth, two with black lines and two with black dots. They "threw" the dice and tallied the wins with tally sticks. They shrieked with laughter when an opponent threw the "four," a combination of the dots and lines. Then the dice were passed on. The young men, interested only in proving their strength and ability, engaged in contests. They jumped against each other, each trying to outdo the mark of the previous jumper, marking the extent of their leaps with sticks. If any man jumped on the stick of an opponent he was disqualified.

They raced, too, laying the track around a pole and back again. Meanwhile, the game of sla hal continued, with the tally sticks moving back and forth between the contestants. The two players were evenly matched, it would seem, for neither had been able to garner all twenty-two sticks. Little groups of old men formed to talk of earlier days and great deeds, while the elder women gossiped, looked after the babies and watched the activity about them.

That evening there was more feasting. Later, when darkness had overtaken the day, the fires were built high and the huge open space was filled with flickering light. The young men piled firewood inside the entry way and took their places at the rear of the house. Cha it zit noticed that they had painted their faces red and black, and that the boxes of dance regalia had been placed nearby.

He heard the sharp rapping of a stick and turned toward the chief's platform to see his father standing there, dressed in his dance attire, a cedar bark headdress, buckskin shirt with small carved clubs sewed on it, and anklets of deer hoof rattles. "Our spirits have returned. They are wanting to *come out*. Now is the time for us to help them." He stooped to pick up his drum and hit a series of short notes. Then he began to drum and to sing. His voice was deep and sonorous, accented by the beat of the drum, it filled the room and vibrated from the walls. Soon others picked up the song, adding their drums and beating sticks to the sound, swelling the volume till it echoed from the very roof boards.

The sound boomed into Cha it zit's ears and filled his whole body. He exulted and thrilled to his father's spirit song; no matter how many times he had heard it before, each performance brought him to new heights.

Then, with the people in full support on their drums, Sax ump ki leaped to the ground and lost himself in the dance. Stooping, leaping, prancing, whirling, always to the incessant beat of the sticks and drums, he danced until his body would allow him to move no more. Then he fell to the ground. At that moment, with a howl, another dancer rose to take his place. The cadence changed, as the dancer had changed, and the people kept pace. Again and again, as one dancer fell, another took his place. Watching the excitement of the *spirit* dances, Cha it zit wondered if he would get a dance and song, too. Then he changed his thinking to when he would be so fortunate as to get a dance, for to be of any account, he must have one.

"It is not over yet," he reminded himself. "The spirit quest is still ahead of me."

The dancing continued far into the night. One by one the children fell asleep wherever they happened to be. The adults, far into the trance that comes when the spirits return, were engrossed in the dances that were being performed. Cha it zit became one with the assemblage, feeling no weariness nor sense of passing time.

The morning was far-spent when the guests and family of Sta nek began to stir. The huge fires of the night before were still burning coals and the women had only to add wood to make them flare again. Wearily, the blanketed forms moved and then rose. The longhouse was a shambles. The floor needed sweeping, possessions were everywhere.

Wanana looked about her, from her sleeping place, in utter dismay. It would take a major effort to put the place in shape again, even to where she and the others could prepare the morning meal.

Cha it zit saw her rise. "I'm glad I'm not a girl," he thought. "It is hard enough being a boy...but a girl? Ugh."

Breakfast was a simple affair. Most of the guests had brought a supply of dried fish and berry cakes which they proceeded to eat.

Then they gathered their possessions to depart. They loaded their gifts into canoes, and with farewells paddled out into the bay, and were soon out of sight.

The village was strangely quiet. Cha it zit and his family wandered back into the empty longhouse. The food storage boxes were mostly empty. There were few furnishings to be seen.

Cha it zit's grandmother spoke. "There will be hunger in our house when the cold winds blow. We will be cold, for many of our blankets are gone."

Wanana soothed the old woman, "It is true, but what a great potlatch we gave. People will know that we are a family to admire, and Cha it zit will receive much respect.

Sax ump ki heard her. "There is still time for us to hunt and fish. We will bring in meat, and furs, too."

"And I can make baskets," Latsi offered. "Grandmother is showing me how."

"Ah, yes, we will manage," Sta nek agreed.

5

Soul Searching

Halibut Hook

The winter was a long, hard one. Rain fell incessantly on the shake roofs of the village houses. There was hunger lurking amid the empty storage boxes and baskets. Children cried for food and the elders, who gave up their own scant rations for them, became pale and gaunt. But no one starved.

Each day a hunting party left the shelter of the houses to search for game. The fishermen, too, braved stormy seas and icy waters to seek a gift of food from the sea. On those scarce days when the sea receded and clam beds were exposed, the women took their digging sticks and sought shellfish.

Sax ump ki, who was known for his hunting skills, spent much of his time in the forest stalking game. Any animal, rabbit, fox, lynx, mountain lion, deer, or elk became his prey. But the creatures of the forest spent much time in their dens and nests, coming out only when hunger drove them. Many days Sax ump ki came back with nothing to put in the cooking boxes.

Cha it zit often accompanied him, not out of choice, but because his father wished him to. He had no desire to become a hunter and feared to attract a hunting spirit. Even though he had been told that each animal he killed would continue to live in his spirit village, the boy felt an aversion to the hunt.

Gradually, the days grew longer. No more did the people rise while it was dark and spend their evenings huddled around fires while the black night moaned and howled outside. The rain softened and there was the smell of spring in the air.

One morning Latsi ran into the longhouse holding a bouquet of salmonberry shoots.

"Here," she called, "see what I found down by the stream."

Cha it zit took a shoot and tasted it. It was tender and sweet, the first green food he had tasted for months.

"When the salmonberry awakens," the elders would say, "all growing things will follow. No longer will the north wind rule the land."

"Soon the ducks will come flying to the north," Sax ump ki announced, "and the herring will come to spawn. The new cycle has begun."

Cha it zit joined the men in the work of preparing the nets to trap the ducks, but his mind was not on the work. The strong nettle webbing had been carefully stored after use the spring before. Now it was taken down from the rafters and tested for weak spots and torn places. While the men worked, deftly replacing worn nettle twine with new material, Cha it zit and his cousins stretched and pulled the nets so that the rips and holes were visible. When the nets had been mended, the boys were sent to cut cedar branches.

"From time beyond recalling," the elders had said, "our ancestors caught ducks in this manner, and added herring roe to their store of food at the same time." The old

men who could no longer hunt and
fish took great pleasure in telling the
village boys how it was done. "We raise the
nets high on poles in places where the ducks
fly by, on a bank above the shore — the same
shore that the herring come to spawn on. Then we
place cedar branches in the water, along the edge,
beneath the net. When the herring come, the female
will choose to lay her eggs on the branches. Now, we
know that ducks love herring eggs, just as we do, so,

when they see the eggs, they fly down for a feast. But instead of eating they become tangled in the net before they can reach the eggs. In the end," the elders would chuckle, "we feast on both ducks and eggs."

As chief hunter, Sax ump ki supervised the raising of the nets. "Erect the poles with the nets tied to them. Now, all together, up!"

The men strained on ropes, and the poles whose butt ends were sitting in deep holes, slowly rose upright. Then the boys quickly filled the post holes with dirt and gravel and trampled the ground around them.

"Good!," Sax ump ki shouted. "Now it is just a matter of waiting. The ducks will come, and our hunger will be appeased."

And the ducks did come. Cha it zit heard them in the night, calling and quacking as they circled and then landed in the water to rest and feed. In the morning the sky was dark with migrating ducks, and the nets were sagging under the weight of those which had flown into them.

"Lower the poles," Sax ump ki ordered.

While the men were pulling down the heavy nets the women brought knives and mats.

"Tonight we will feast," they laughed excitedly. "Our bellies will be full at last. The hungry times are behind us now."

Fires were started in a long, quickly dug trench on the gravel beach. Using alder, prized for its slow even burning which produced glowing coals, the women tended the fires. All of the villagers gathered about the fire pits, anticipating the feast of fresh barbecued duck.

When the coals in the trench were deep and glowing, the ducks were impaled on sharpened sticks thrust into their skulls and propped over the fire to roast.

Cha it zit, perched on a small knoll above the beach, watched the scene below. He could see his brother, Cha wentz, and several of the other young warriors gathered in a group to one side of the fire trench. They each carried a spear and jade blades were thrust through their belts. Their bodies were hard and lean and when they moved, it was with assurance.

"They will eat first," Cha it zit knew. "It is important that the warriors are strongest," he had been told. "Others must sacrifice, for their power defends us."

Cha it zit thought about Cha wentz, watching him there, so strong, so confident. He and his older brother had not been close, even when they were younger and no great gulf separated them. "Maybe it was because our different mothers were not friendly to each other," he mused. Cha wentz's mother was the first wife to Sax ump ki, and as such she held a high position. But Wanana was his favorite, and the other wives envied her. "If my father had not had four wives, maybe we could have been closer. Latsi is my own true sister, and I am lucky to have her, but now, I wish I could know Cha wentz better. Maybe, now that I have a great name, and am soon to be a man, he will accept me," Cha it zit considered, hopefully.

Even as he longed to be close to Cha wentz, Cha it zit was envious of his prestige as a warrior, and his arrogance. He wondered how it felt to have the spirit power to become a warrior, to have everyone look up to you, to admire and fear you.

"But I don't want to be a warrior," he told himself. "They are like hunters who stalk and kill. I don't want to get a warrior spirit."

He worried about what spirit he would find, or even more troublesome, what spirit would find him. But the day was too special to allow such thoughts to spoil it for long.

The ducks were beginning to roast and the smell was wafting up to him in a tantalizing aroma. His mouth watered and his empty belly ached for the food. Then the awful thought came; "Would Sax ump ki allow him to eat?" Since the naming, Sax ump ki had increased the trials of training, and Cha it zit was often denied even the scanty rations available to the others.

Below him, the women had brought water buckets and dippers so that all might drink before eating. Little children were playing around their mothers, begging for morsels like so many puppies while the elders sat on mats waiting expectantly about the fires.

At last the call came, "The ducks are ready." Cha it zit watched the villagers converge at the fire pit. They waited until the women had removed the ducks from the spits and placed them on cattail mats.

Then the warriors came forward and, without ceremony, each grabbed a duck and carried it to a place away from the milling people. Then the elders, followed by men of various professions, picked up their ducks and retired to mats to eat. Then women and children, boys and girls snatched their food and began to tear at the flesh hungrily.

Eating the ducks was a simple process since the heat of the fire had burned off most of the feathers and those that were left came off with the skin when it was pulled away from the flesh.

The spring feast of fresh meat continued until the last duck had been consumed and the people lay about, satiated to the point of stupefaction.

Cha it zit had his fill, too. No one interfered or told him he must not eat, or demanded that he vomit what he had consumed. He ate a whole duck and returned for more. How many? He lost count — was it three, four? His stomach rebelled at the quantity and the richness of the oily meat. A terrible pain began in his abdomen and pushed up into his throat. He laid on the ground and rolled. It didn't help.

"Oh-h-h," he groaned. "Why didn't father stop me? I am being punished for my gluttony. Oh-h-h, hunger was better than this."

Some of the men were sleeping. A few of the young women were making a half-hearted effort to clean up the carcasses and duck bones that had been strewn about. Dogs darted in, whining and snarling, to grab the remains, and then dart out again with their prizes. Sleep came to Cha it zit, too, and eased his torture. All became quiet, except for the scuffling dogs who finished the feast, to the last bone.

The herring came, as the people knew they would, and laid their eggs on the cedar branches. Wave after wave of ducks arrived. Spotting the tempting roe, they dove for it, only to become tangled in the nets. Each day Cha it zit and the other boys gathered the ducks and brought them to the women. They were boiled in a soup, baked in a pit, cooked on a stick, or dried in the sun.

Greens were sprouting in the clearings — fern fiddleheads, wild celery, offering vitamins and minerals. There was food to be had, in abundance, at last.

When the ducks had passed on their flight to the north the herring roe was gathered, still on the branches. Then the women built smoky fires and set the branches above them. Cha it zit watched as Latsi and Wanana tended the roe, turning the branches as it smoked and hardened. At last the delicacy was ready.

Seeing her brother, Latsi tore a string of the roe, now firm and brown from the smoke, and handed it to him when no one was looking. Cha it zit took it eagerly. He relished the rich, smokey taste of the roe. The goodness of it rolled on his palate. He savored it, and remembering the torture he had endured when he over-ate the first ducks of

the season, he chewed slowly. But, like all rich foods, the roe lay heavy in his stomach which was still sensitive because of his continual state of semi-starvation. But to the boy it was a small price to pay for the pleasure he had derived from the treat.

When quantities of the herring roe had been processed and stored in baskets for winter use the people turned to food gathering in earnest. For the next six months they would be wholly occupied in the down-to-earth task of gathering and storing great quantities of food. Their quest would take them to the nearby islands for camas bulbs and spring salmon. Then they would travel farther, back to the island of Al lu lung for clams and the small deer that lived there. The runs of the five great tribes of the *salmon people* would keep the fishermen busy until fall. Netting, trapping, trolling, spearing, the men would bring hoards of salmon. For endless days the smoking-drying fires would smolder while the women cleaned, split and hung the rich, red-fleshed fish. When the process was completed, the hard smoked fish would be stored, looking like slabs of wood, in baskets until they were needed during the dark, cold winter days.

Later, the people would journey up the great Neutsack river to gather huckleberries and blueberries on the slopes of the great mountains. The mountains were fearful places, with their tops lost in clouds. Above them all, rising as a dome into the sky, stood Kulshan, the most powerful being of that wild country. From his crest smoke would rise and the elders would tell of times, long ago, when his anger was so terrible that fire and black smoke shot from him, and ashes covered the whole countryside. Then it was dark for days, with no sunshine. Even the birds hushed their twittering. Sometimes lightening and thunder would emanate from the mountain, and one could hear the roar of a thousand drums as snow rushed down its slopes. It was with good reason that the people feared the terror of the mountains. But they needed the food that was there, not only the berries, but the meat of the deer, the elk and the bear. The women treasured the wool of the mountain goat, which they gathered from branches where it had been torn from the coat of a passing animal. Blankets woven from mountain goat wool were warm and valuable. So, taking their fear with them, the bravest hunters and their wives ventured into the high country. Later, around the winter fires, they would tell of their great exploits in the land of the mountain spirits.

It was not until the leaves began to fall that the people could return to their permanent village and rest. If they had been successful in their quest for food, there would be feasting and plenty in the longhouses. If not, they would be hungry before the long winter had come to an end.

Cha it zit knew the routine. He had participated in it for several years, ever since that proud day when his father had said, "Oogli is old enough. No longer will he remain in the village with the elders. He will learn to fish and hunt. When he becomes a man he must know these things."

The preparations for travel were underway. Cha it zit watched the women mending mats that would become temporary shelters. Then they repacked food boxes and made storage baskets to hold the stock of food they would bring back. The men, meantime, worked over their nets, patching holes, and replacing worn parts. They tested their fishlines of nettle and cedar bark, checked their spears, clubs, arrows and fish hooks. Cha it zit was called upon to run errands, bring materials, and to perform countless small tasks. He did it all willingly, since to complain would reflect on his worthiness and ability to get a great spirit gift.

The time was drawing near when the canoes would be loaded and one by one the families would leave. Cha it zit pondered the decision he must make. He was needed to help bring in food, he knew, but he also knew that the time was approaching when he must set out alone to seek his *gift*. He could feel something deep inside himself urging him to act — to go.

"My body is ready," he told himself, tensing his lean sinewy body, "but my mind is not. I am afraid to go," he admitted.

"How can I be sure that I will get the *spirit* that I want?" he wondered, as he had so many times in the past. Cha it zit knew that sometimes spirits would come looking for people to enter — not always desirable spirits, either. "My father is a great warrior," he mused. "His power is so great that no man fears to do battle when he is present. My brother has a warrior spirit, too, and everyone fears and respects him. But one thing that I know, I don't want such a power and I don't want to attract such a spirit. I don't want to be a great hunter, either, I do not wish to kill. I know that I could help my people and they would think well of me if I was able to bring much food to them. I have heard that a hunter with a strong spirit can will the game to come to him and wish to be slain. That is a wonderful thing, but not for me. There are fishermen among our people who tell how the fish will leap into their boats, their power is so great. It must be so, for they always bring back a large catch, and all the villagers eat because of them."

Cha it zit's mind raced on, exploring all the possible sources of spirit power, and always it came back to rest on an unusual thought. He would remember how he watched the gamblers as they played sla hal at his naming potlatch. The game had fascinated him, and the fascination had remained as intense as when he had first fallen under its spell. Suddenly he knew what sort of power he would seek.

"I want to be a great gambler," he thought with a shock. "I want to be the head of a great house, to be wealthy and to be known as a gifted sla hal player. Yes, that is what I want. All men will respect me for I shall have a great skill. And my skill at the game will bring me wealth and fame. With my wealth I can help my people – that will be as important as bringing them fish and game, or winning battles." His imagination rushed on. "Yes. I shall be known to all the villages as Cha it zit, a great siem, a man to be respected."

It was decided. But how to find such a spirit to help him achieve his goal! He remembered the old shaman Tselique. Two times the ancient medicine man had befriended him when he was in need. Cha it zit fingered the raven amulet which always hung about his neck in the leather pouch that Latsi had made for him. "Perhaps he will

consent to advise me, to tell me what I must do to attract a gambling spirit, but no other."

Cha it zit was elated — his mind soared to encompass this new reality. He had made a decision. His spirit quest was to be soon, and he knew what he wanted. For the first time in his life, he actively sought his father. "It's not that I don't respect my father," he reasoned, analyzing his feelings, "I do, maybe more than anyone else. But I think I fear him more than I love him. I wish that I could measure up to his expectations for me, but I cannot and still be faithful to my dream for myself. I admire him, but I don't want to be like him, that much I know." Somehow, Cha it zit felt, he would have to try to make Sax ump ki know how he felt about his spirit quest, about his newfound understanding of himself and his life-goal.

He found Sax ump ki supervising the preparation of the canoes for traveling. He and the other men of the village had piled planks on the beach near the large traveling canoes. Strong cedarbark ropes lay in coils, ready for use. Cha it zit waited until his father noticed him standing there.

"Ha, Cha it zit," he called, speaking the name distinctly and with care. "Come and give us a hand. We will lash these planks across two canoes to make a raft to carry our equipment and supplies."

The boy stepped forward to do as he had been asked. For some time he worked alongside the men, pushing, carrying, tugging, lashing. At last Sa ump ki called a halt. "We have done enough, it is time to rest."

"Father," Cha it zit took hold of the opportunity, "I would talk with you. I need your advice."

"And you shall have it," Sax ump ki responded, smiling and pleased that his son had approached him. "Sit here beside me on this log and we will talk. What do you wish to talk about?"

"I must ask leave to go. It is time — I feel it within myself — to make my spirit quest."

"You are young," Sax ump ki replied thoughtfully, "but I, too, think you are ready. You have trained hard. You have learned much. Your body has become hardened to pain and privation. Your mind has sharpened. You may go when you wish."

"There is more," Cha it zit continued. "I know what spirit I will seek, but I do not know its name or how to find it. I only want one kind of power."

"It is a fortunate boy who knows what he wants," Sax ump ki ventured, looking out toward the distant islands that lay beyond the bay.

"I don't want to displease you, father," Cha it zit said in a low, hesitant voice, "but the gift I seek is not the gift of a great hunter or warrior like you. It has come to me that I am different from you or Cha wentz."

Sax ump ki heard this and looked thoughtfully at his younger son. For a long time boy and man sat side by side on the log and stared silently across the water. The sun dropped lower over the islands and the sky deepened to mauve, then streaks of gold and then vanished into night.

Cha it zit, fearing he had offended his father dared not speak. "Let him approve of my desire," he wished. At last Sa ump ki turned to his son.

"I had hoped that you would pursue a strong spirit such as I have. There is much I would teach you and give to you. But it has become obvious to me during the months of your training that you do not want such a spirit. Yes, I knew it long before you told me of it, but I had hoped that you would change. That is why I pushed you so hard, why I challenged you so often, why I deprived you to build up your resolve and your ability to withstand punishment."

"All that you have done was for my good," Cha it zit assured him. "If you did not want the best for me you would not have cared so much, and tried so hard. Then he paused as a thought came to him. "Do you remember when you sent me to see the old shaman, Tselique? He told me many things. One thought that he gave to me was that I should be true to myself, to what I saw as being right for me. That I have tried to do. I do not want to hurt or disappoint you, but I must follow my own feelings in this quest."

"Then I must warn you. You must take care that such a spirit as I possess does not find you. Since the warrior spirits come freely to me, you must separate yourself from me until your quest is over. Even then you may not be safe. It is not uncommon for men to have more than one spirit...spirits they did not seek and did not want, and which caught them and dominated them for their own ends."

"But I will need your counsel," Cha it zit remonstrated.

"You will have counsel," his father assured him. "I will summon Tselique. He has served you well before, he will serve you now. He will tell you those things you will need to know. Leave me now."

Cha it zit did not see his father again before the family departed in search of the year's supply of food.

From a vantage point on a bluff some distance from the village the boy watched the final preparations. He saw those who would be going, the strong ones and the slaves who would do much of the menial work, the women and older girls who would process the foods. His father loomed over the others, taller, heavier, aristocratic in bearing. He easily dominated the scene. Cha it zit always felt pride when he looked at Sax ump ki. Born and bred of the nobility, the chief of all the villages of Lummi, Sax ump ki commanded the respect of all who knew him, particularly of his younger son.

Then Cha it zit saw his mother. Petite, she looked like a child standing beside her husband. Of his four wives,

Cha it zit had long ago sensed that Wanana held Sax ump ki's heart, and that he and Latsi were closer to him than his other children.

Cha wentz was preparing to launch a canoe in which he would travel with his mother and younger brother. The other wives were readying their canoes, ordering their slaves and children.

"I should be there," Cha it zit thought, "to help mother. But my time has come."

Then he saw a small figure break away from the group and run up the beach toward him. It was Latsi. Cha it zit heard Wanana call after her, but the girl would not stop.

"Oogli," she cried, using the old pet name. "Oogli, won't you come with us? Please come."

"Latsi," he shouted, "go back, they will be angry with you. Everyone is ready to go." He ran down the hill toward her.

Latsi was breathless and her large eyes were filled with tears. Cha it zit put his hands on her shoulders. "It is time for me to go on my quest," he told her. "If I go with the others I will not return for many moons. Perhaps it will be too late then, the cold rains will have already come. You must go without me, little sister. When you return perhaps I will be a man."

"Or you may be dead," she answered, ruefully. "Many boys never return when they go out."

"If that is my fate, so be it," Cha it zit said, "but I'll tell you, Latsi, I will not die easily. Do not worry. When you return I'll be here waiting." He pushed her gently and added, "Now go, before you get into serious trouble."

The girl turned and fled back to the waiting canoes. One by one they left the shelter of the beach. Cha it zit noticed with satisfaction that Sax ump ki took his place in the stern of Wanana's canoe and sent it flying with a strong thrust of his paddle. He could see Latsi's small form amid the baggage.

The elders, standing at the doors of their houses, waved and watched till the canoes and freight-carrying rafts were well out into the swift running water of the strait.

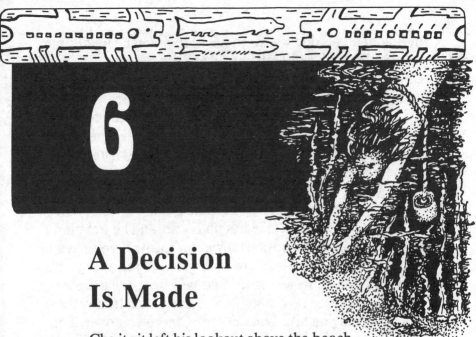

6

A Decision Is Made

Cha it zit left his lookout above the beach and walked back to his family's longhouse. He would bring in wood and carry water for his grandmother, he thought, and then choose a canoe from those belonging to Sax ump ki.

As he neared the house he heard a familiar voice. "Ah, here is the boy they call Cha it zit. I would speak with him."

Turning, the boy spied Tselique, the old shaman, hobbling toward him. He looked tired and older than Cha it zit remembered him.

"I am happy to see you," Cha it zit greeted him.

"Ah, yes, it is good to see you, too. But I am here at your father's request. You need advice and counsel, I am told, on the quest you will soon undertake."

"I need to know how to get the spirit I desire," Cha it zit explained.

"There are many spirits," the old man said, thoughtfully. "Each one has its own ways—ways you must learn if you would be sure to find the one you want and avoid finding one you don't wish to have. If you will sit with me here on this rock I will tell you what I can."

Together, the ancient man and the boy, soon to be a man, sat on a moss covered rock in the sunshine.

"Now," Tselique began, "You must not tell me what you see — not now or ever. If you do, you will give me power over you...power that I do not wish to have. Just listen to me and choose for yourself what you must do."

Cha it zit nodded.

"Many boys desire to become great warriors. Sqaip is a powerful war spirit. He has no house, and he travels all the time looking for boys who want a spirit. If you have a vision of him, you will know for he is painted red all over his head and body. He will say, 'You will be a great fighter. When you dance, take a knife and cut yourself and show how powerful you are. Look at me! I am red all over. That is blood, not paint. These wounds do not hurt me. You will be the same,'" Tselique touched Cha it zit's shoulder. "If you get this spirit you will be able to dance on fire. You will be a great warrior, as your father and brother are."

"Tell me of others," Cha it zit requested. "If you would be a great fisherman, Tcadzo is a spirit to look for. It stays under water all the time, in a river or the salt water. To find it you must go in a canoe and search and wait. It looks like a decoy for ducks."

"What other spirits are there?"

"There are spirits for getting wealth and property," the shaman told him.

"I wish to know about them," Cha it zit tried not to show the keen interest that he felt, but his voice quavered and he wondered if Tselique noticed.

"Heyida lives in a large house which is filled with many valuable things. He owns many slaves and is very wealthy. He looks like a person, but he does not walk or use a canoe, instead he flies through the air. If you seek him you can do it on the land. He travels about and also sends messengers to find boys, like you, of high blood. If you find the Heyida spirit, it will say to you 'You will become wealthy, because of me. You will not have to work, for others will do that for you.' He will give you a song. For a while you will hear the song in your mind day and night."

"You said there were spirits for gaining wealth," Cha it zit turned to look at Tselique. "Are there other spirits beside Heyida?"

"There is Tiolbax." The old man appeared to be hesitating.

"What of it?" Cha it zit wanted to know, his eyes shining with interest.

"It is more powerful than Heyida, but it is also more difficult to find. This spirit will cause neighboring tribes to bring gifts to the owner. Whoever finds Tiolbax may have many wives, because other men will bring their daughters for him to marry and not even ask a price for them. It is a great honor to have someone with Tiolbax in the family. That spirit has many powers, even causing game to drop dead at the door of those who have *found* it."

"Would the Tiolbax spirit help a man win at sla hal?" Cha it zit wanted to know.

"Yes, of course, if that is what the owner wanted," Tselique replied.

"And how does one find this spirit?"

"It is not easy. It lives under the sea in deep water. Tiolbax has a longhouse which is filled with much wealth and property. To find him one must dive with a stone."

"How is that done?" the boy wanted to know.

"It is difficult. Many die trying for this spirit. That is why there are very few men who have had the power of the Tiolbax. I have hesitated to even tell you of this spirit. The quest is dangerous, but the rewards are great to those who are successful."

"Tell me how one seeks the Tiolbax," Cha it zit's tone became demanding.

"If you have a canoe, that is best. If not, make yourself a raft. Fasten a very long cedar rope to it. Now, take a heavy rock and cover it with saliva. That will help to protect you from harm. Tie the rope to yourself and holding the rock, jump into deep ocean water. The rock will take you down farther than you could dive where the water is black and cold. Look around you. If you see a longhouse, you will have found Tiolbax. I do not know what will happen then. As I said before, very few men have ever found that spirit. If you do not see a house, drop the rock and follow the rope to the surface. You may need to do this many times. Sometimes the vision will only come when you have exhausted yourself and are about to die. Sometimes the vision may never come at all. One would be well advised to seek another vision."

"Can you tell me more about the quest for Tiolbax?" Cha it zit pursued. He was filled with an inner excitement that was visible in his tense body.

The shaman nodded understandingly. "I have been told that it is wise to hide a sharp stick in your hair in case there are harmful creatures in the deep water."

"You have told me much," Cha it zit said. "I am grateful. Now go to the longhouse and you can take your ease at my grandmother's fire. She might brew some tea for you." The old man ambled off and the boy ran toward a small canoe that lay at anchor, gently rocking in the waves. Cha it zit leaped into the craft, pulled up the anchoring rock and, grabbing a paddle, made for the open water of the bay. He was elated.

At last he knew the identity of the spirit he would seek. He even knew how to look for it, how to attract its attention. All that remained, he reasoned, was the actual act of going after the power he desired.

Cha it zit paddled furiously, senselessly, expending his energy on the sea. The canoe responded by leaping through the water.

Finally he tired, and laying his paddle across his knees, Cha it zit let the boat drift, rising and falling as a sea bird does when it rests on the waves. The shore was a blue haze in the distance and he was completely alone.

"This is the way it will be when I go out," he thought. "Just me alone. Whatever I do, I must do by myself. It will be my body, my strength and my courage against all the forces of nature. But I can do it!! I know I can...and get the Tiolbax spirit power."

He noticed that the sun was beginning to near the horizon, so, reluctantly, he swung the canoe around and began the long trip home.

It was almost dark when Cha it zit entered the long-house. His grandmother was busy at the cooking fire, heating water with white-hot rocks for the evening meal of duck soup. Tselique was nowhere to be seen, but Sta nek was sitting on his platform. He rose and called out, "I have heard that you are going soon."

"Yes, Grandfather, I feel the need to go."

"It is good, the time is right. I hear, also, that you have in mind the spirit you will seek." The old man held up his hand as Cha it zit was about to speak. "Do not tell me its name. Always keep that to yourself, even after you have obtained the power you seek."

"I know, the shaman has warned me."

"I want you to have this," Sta nek said, taking an amulet from around his neck. Cha it zit knew it well – a small bone carving of a blackfish. As long as he could remember the old man had worn it. Now it was to be his. His grandfather hung the charm, suspended on a leather thong, around Cha it zit's neck where it rested beside the sack holding the raven charm. "This will protect you, as it has protected me. It was given to me by my own grandfather when I was about your age, preparing for my quest."

"I am proud to wear it," the boy said, simply.

"Where will you go?"

"What I seek is in the sea. I will go to the place of our ancestors, to the waters beside Al lu lung."

"Ah. I know them well. They are cold and deep and treacherous, those waters. The open sea boils through them on its journey into our inland waters. There are whirlpools in which forces dwell...forces that will swallow a large canoe and all its occupants. I tremble for your safety. Many who seek spirits of the sea do not return."

"I know that, Grandfather. But that is where I must seek. This amulet will help to keep me safe." Cha it zit ran his finger around the contours of the blackfish, feeling the patina, worn smooth by the touch of those who had worn it before.

"True. And I will ask Tselique to use his powers to protect you as well."

"Tselique. Does someone mention that name?" came a voice from behind some storage boxes in a dark recess of the great house.

"Ah, my brother, you have been listening. Come out, we have need of your magic," Sta nek called.

There was a stirring, a moving of boxes, and the shaman appeared, slowly making his way toward the old chief's platform. Cha it zit moved to make room for Tselique on the bench beside Sta nek.

"Tonight I will invoke the spirits that serve me. They will form a cloak of safety around this young lad."

"You would do well, brother, for I feel deep within myself that the future well-being of our people may depend upon Cha it zit," Sta nek commented.

"I see in him qualities of leadership which go beyond the ability to wield a war club. I am old, I have lived long,

maybe too long, but my mind goes back to my own youth
when I look at Cha it zit, I see myself in him."

"The soup is ready," Tseutsi called. All conversation
halted for the one large meal of the day. The hearty soup,
laced with seaweed and greens, tasted good to Cha it zit. He
was allowed to eat his fill. "This will be my last meal until I
receive my gift," he thought. A second thought entered his
mind, uninvited. "This may be the last meal I ever eat if I
fail—for I will never give up until I die."

"You leave in the morning." His grandfather voiced
his words more as a statement than a question.

"Yes," Cha it zit answered, hardly realizing that he
had actually committed himself to going.

Tseutsi rummaged through her storage boxes and
found several cakes of dried berries and bear tallow. She
handed them to the boy.

"Take these," she said. "It will not hurt for you to take nourishment on your way."

"No," Tselique said, taking the cakes from her. "To do so would only delay the vision he is seeking. The spirit he wants is the hardest of all to get. He must deprive himself, as he has learned to do. He must know hunger and thirst and cold until his soul is ready to leave his body. Then, and only then, the vision will come, if he is worthy to receive such a gift."

Woodworking Tools
Maul, Adze, Chisel

The Quest

Before the dawn, before the old people of the house had risen, Cha it zit was up. He took his fur robe from his bed, a cattail rain cape, his spear, a knife, a stout rope and several rush mats. These he carried to the small canoe he had chosen. He silently pushed away from the shore.

His route lay around the island called Lummi, past several smaller islands where camas beds lay. He would travel by traditional salmon trolling and reef netting areas. He hoped that he would not see his tribesmen or his family along the way. Cha it zit felt the need to be alone.

As he rounded the northern tip of Lummi he could see fishermen working from their canoes in the distance. It was easy to avoid them. Farther along, as he skirted one of the small islands, he could hear the sound of women's voices as they laughed and gossiped while digging the sweet camas bulb. Cha it zit slid silently past them.

Ahead loomed the bulk of Al lu lung, its peak shrouded in clouds. He thought of the first man to come

115

there. "He found his home and his power there. His descendants, including me, became a great people, the Lummis. So I will go back to that source to find my own power and my place among my people." Cha it zit was pleased by the logic of his choice and his confidence about the outcome of his quest rose. He was eager to meet the challenge.

The hours passed. The sun had risen to its height in the sky and was declining. He was becoming very tired. Hard as his body had become, strong as his back and arms were, he had reached the limits of his ability. A small island, more of an outcropping of rocks, lay to his right. "This may be a place where I can tie the canoe and rest," he thought. The sun was now dipping toward the horizon or distant islands and soon it would be dark. Slipping between rocky sentinels, he found a tiny beach shaded by an ancient madrona tree which sprawled toward the water.

Once the canoe was tied to the tree's trunk, Cha it zit laid face down on the cool, damp sand. His body seemed to sink into the ground, so tired was he. It was not so much sleep as oblivion. He lay senseless until the morning sun brought him back to reality.

His body ached, but more than that, he realized a terrible pain in his abdomen. "I am hungry," he thought realizing that he hadn't eaten for a day and a night. "A man can resist hunger," Cha it zit told himself. Dragging himself to the waters edge, he pulled the canoe toward him, stepped in and paddled toward the looming mountain of Al lu lung.

Toward noon he reached the swift running straits which led toward the open sea. That was when the awful reality of what he was doing really penetrated his consciousness. This was to be a serious effort, filled with danger and a very real chance that he might not survive. He had trained long and hard for this day, but now that the moment had come an overpowering fear gripped him. Cha it zit was glad that he was alone. To have others see his terror, his weakness, would have been unbearable to him. The canoe swung and lurched in the fast-running tide. Small whirlpools threatened to engulf his fragile craft. He pulled hard until he reached slick water, running cold and black.

"Here," he said aloud. "Here I will try."

Mechanically, he made the preparations — tie his rope to the canoe prow through the hole provided for anchoring. Tie the other end around his waist — the long rope should let him down many feet into the depths of the water. Spit on the rock and smear the saliva around for protection. Put a sharpened stick he had prepared into his hair. Instinctively, he felt for the shaman's amulet and his grandfather's charm which hung about his neck. As he did so, their kindly, concerned faces appeared in his mind and Cha it zit felt a sense of protection.

"I am ready," he announced to the seabirds that circled overhead. That is when he saw the lone black raven flying above him.

"Raven," he called, pleading in his voice. "Help me!"

"Caaaaaaa." The bird's answer rang clear as it circled lower over the canoe.

Then Cha it zit dove into the water. It was cold beyond belief — and grew even colder as he sank quickly, pulled down by the heavy rock. Down — down to where it was black as night, he dropped. He felt that his lungs would burst, but still he sank. His ears rang and he felt that sounds were coming to him from the depths below, but they held no meaning. Then he ceased to think...he was in a void...his body no longer seemed to exist.

That was when, from somewhere, a warning came. "Drop the rock — climb the rope — now!"

How he did it, Cha it zit didn't know. Somehow he rose toward the light, and at last, to the air. Clinging to the side of his canoe, which was canting crazily in the turbulent water, he gasped great gulps of air into his starved lungs. He was too weak to climb into the boat, but as his mind began to clear he realized that he could not remain in the cold water any longer.

The shaman's face came to him again, and he responded to an inner urging. Lifting himself with his arms, he was able to swing his torso over the side of the canoe and to steady it by thrusting with his feet until he could pull one leg and then the other over the side of the canoe.

There had been no vision, and Cha it zit knew that he had barely survived the dive. He was disappointed and dejected. He lay down in the bottom of the boat and looked up at the sky. Little white clouds, fed by the moisture of the sea, were forming. He did not see the raven, only flocks of wheeling gulls. The boy wondered, "Can I do it again? Knowing the cold and blackness of the water, the possibility of death that lies there?" He must, he knew, if he was to get the Tiolbax spirit. There was no other way.

When he had recovered somewhat, he took another stone, prepared himself and dove again. After that dive, he vomited and lay in the canoe, trembling. He pulled his robe over him and warmed his body.

Over and over, Cha it zit dove, and always, he did not know how, he managed to reach the surface in time to revive himself.

That night he slept in the canoe, letting it drift with the current. The next day he dove again. It became routine. Dive. Recover. Dive. Recover. His senses were dulled as the self-inflicted torture continued.

At last the time came when the boy was forced to realize that his strength was gone, and that he could not survive another dive, and that no vision had come to him. He was defeated. He had no hope left of finding Tiolbax. He had failed in the one great endeavor of his life, he was

118

not worthy, and in his own eyes and those of his people he would be of no value.

He wondered if he should return to his village. He could do as the original man had done, land on Al lu lung and remain there hiding from his own people. There was food to sustain him, he could survive.

Then he thought of Latsi, of her faith in him, and of his promise to her: "I'll be waiting for you when you come back." How could he never see her again? He could see her face, looking at him the way she did, admiration in her eyes. Then another face appeared in his mind, the face of the girl he had seen at his naming. He would never see her again, never get to know her. That seemed to be very important to him and he wondered about it. In fact, he admitted, he had thought about her quite often. Strange. He realized that he had to go home. Could he fake a vision? Tell his father that he had found a spirit gift. He wasn't supposed to tell what it was. Who would know? Then he remembered the shaman's warning and the story of the *false squedelich*, the man who tried that. No, Cha it zit knew he had to be truthful. "Perhaps I could find a lesser spirit helper," he considered. "After all, I chose to find the most difficult one of all. Hardly anyone has a Tiolbax. Tselique knew of only a few men who did."

Almost without thinking, the exhausted boy began to paddle. It had been five days since he had eaten or had a drink and his strength had left him. Slowly the beaches and trees of Al lu lung began to fade as he moved away toward the islands that sheltered the mainland and the Lummi villages. After a while he laid his paddle down and slipped into a state of semi-consciousness. The canoe continued on its way, as if propelled by an unseen force. In the dim recesses of his mind Cha it zit recalled the time he had been sent to the small island to meet the shaman. Then, too, when he was tired beyond endurance, the canoe had guided itself. "The spirit of the sea is doing it," he concluded, "I do have a helper."

Cha it zit lost consciousness. He was aware, yet not responsive to his situation. He was content to drift, to let the spirit forces direct his fate. He no longer cared, or cared to act. So through the day and the night the canoe drifted with its passenger more a corpse than a living body, lying prone under the bear fur rug.

Toward dawn, when the first light was glowing gold across the sky, reflecting itself on the ripples of the water that lapped gently against the canoe, Cha it zit roused himself with a start.

Something strange had happened. The canoe had struck an object in the water just below the surface. The hull had scraped along what seemed to be boards and now the craft was grounded, grating against whatever was under it. Cha it zit peered over and down into the water. To his amazement he saw that it was indeed boards — actually a roof. The canoe was sitting on the roof of a large longhouse under the water. Then he heard a voice calling to him.

"I am he who you seek! The spirit called Tiolbax. Your power will be in your house, as mine is in my house. It is through your house, which will be great, that you will gain wealth and prestige."

"Tiolbax," Cha it zit shouted. At the sound of his voice a raven cawed and the boy turned to see it soaring high overhead.

Cha it zit felt suddenly strong. He felt powerful. His soul expanded in him till he felt he would burst with happiness — more than happiness, relief, fulfillment, satisfaction. He had found his spirit power. His quest was completed. He had succeeded!

"I accept your gift," he called out to Tiolbax, "and I am grateful."

When he looked around him, he saw, to his amazement, that he was almost home. The morning was bright and he felt new-born. As he picked up his paddle to return to the village, a song began to come to him. At first it was only a hint, but the beat and the tune grew until he was compelled to sing it. He beat the time with his paddle and began to sing out loud as the words came.

"I found it
it is mine
it spoke
it is mine
it is power
it is mine
it is wealth
it is mine."

The song dominated him. All else left his mind. The canoe, carried by the incoming tide, drifted toward shore.

Something moved on the hilltop above the beach, the place where Cha it zit went when he needed to be alone, to think. At first, when he noticed it, the boy thought that it was an old blanket moving with the wind. But as he watched, the blanket seemed to unfold and to slowly rise. Then Cha it zit recognized Tselique as he began to stiffly make his way down the steep slope. The song still possessed Cha it zit, it would not release him, so he continued to sing and to beat his paddle as if it were a live thing.

He saw Tselique coming across the beach. It seemed as if it was a dream, he came so slowly. At times he seemed to fade away entirely, to be lost in a swirl of wind, and then he would materialize in another place. Cha it zit could not tell whether the shaman's feet were actually on the beach stones, or floating a few inches above. He tried to catch the expression on Tselique's weatherbeaten and incredibly wrinkled face, but his features seemed to be constantly moving about.

As the boy sang, Tselique slowly and cautiously approached the drifting canoe. It was only a few feet from shore, gently rocking in the wind.

When he was almost there, Tselique stopped, drew a charm from the bag he carried suspended from his waist, and began to sing in a quavering voice. He fingered the small ivory carving and danced a few mincing steps.

Then, still singing he approached the canoe.

Cha it zit became quiet. The song died in his throat. He stared at Tselique, seeing him, but yet not seeing him.

Raven

8

It Is Over

"Oogli...Cha it zit," Tselique said, almost in a whisper, "come, it is over." "Tselique" was the only word that would come from the boy's parched throat. He tried to rise, to leave the canoe, but his body would not respond.

"It is understandable," Tselique told him, "your body has been severely tested...you must be patient with it. Here, let me help you."

The old shaman held out a claw-like hand. Cha it zit placed his own roughened, calloused hand in it. He felt a current run through him and his body moved. The two of them, the emaciated old man and the exhausted youth slowly made their way up the worn path to the village.

"There will be talk later," Tselique said. "First you must regain your strength.

"But one thing I must warn you about. Do not tell anyone of the thing that has happened. If you do, the power may leave you. I know more than you realize, but even so, don't tell me the exact nature of your spirit gift. Let it rest in you, make you its home for now."

With each step Cha it zit seemed to gain strength, but strangely, so did Tselique seem to weaken.

"He is here! He is here!" a child called out. Moments later Cha it zit and Tselique were surrounded by the small children of the village.

"Did you find it?" one small boy wanted to know.

"What was it like?" another asked.

"Ooooh, you look awful," a girl remarked with a grimace.

"Run along, bring Sta nek," Tselique ordered them. The children, fearful of the old shaman, ran off to find Cha it zit's grandfather while the pair slowly made their way to the family longhouse. They were met at the low entrance by Sta nek who was panting, evidently having run from wherever it was that the children had found him.

"My spirit is glad that you have returned, Grandson," he said as he placed a hand on Cha it zit's shoulder. "We will present ourselves to your grandmother and perhaps she will make some nettle soup to warm you and give strength to your belly."

When Tseutsi saw them enter, she arose from her place by the family hearth to greet Cha it zit. Carefully giving him the respect of distance now that he had become a man in the eyes of the community, she spoke.

"I am happy for your safe return, my Grandson. Do sit and I will serve you for I perceive that you are in need of nourishment."

Cha it zit would have rushed to her as he had done in the old days, but he remembered his new station and his body was reluctant to move. "It is odd," he thought, "to be considered a man but to think of myself as unchanged. This will take some adjustment."

The three sat on mats which Tseutsi provided and waited as she busied herself building up the coals into a small cooking fire.

Cha it zit seemed to go into a reverie as he watched the flames leap to consume the kindling of cedar twigs and then grow into the strength of a full fire. "Is life like that?" he wondered. "We carefully nurture our fire and it grows until at last it consumes us?" He looked at Tselique — so ancient had he grown. He wondered if Tselique's fire, his power, was consuming him. "Will my new-found power consume me?" It was a terrible thought and he let it slip away.

Now Tseutsi was placing her cooking rocks close beside the fire to heat until they glowed a dull red.

Sta nek had been regarding Cha it zit. "I see, Grandson, that you have suffered. I also feel that your quest has been successful. There is something different about you. Some new dimension has been added. You are not ready to speak of it yet... and so I will not ask you. Hunger and thirst have left their mark on you, too. Now you must bring yourself back slowly and carefully. Your grandmother will know how to help you. Do as she says. And," he turned to Tselique, "my brother, you too need care. I know it to be true that you have not eaten since Cha it zit left. Both of you must gain strength."

Tselique nodded and replied, "The boy needed my help."

"So," Cha it zit thought, "Tselique had been with me all the time, with me in his spirit body." He remembered the times when he must have been feeling the Shaman's thoughts, when the canoe seemed to propel itself, when some power sustained him, even when the raven appeared. It began to come clear to him. This quest had not been his alone. Strange feelings surfaced. He felt gratitude, but resentment, too. Why couldn't he have done it without any help?

Tselique seemed to read his thoughts. "There is much that you do not know, my nephew, much that is yet to be revealed to you. Do not fret. Yours was a true vision, the result of a great experience. What I did only helped to clear the way and to sustain you until you could complete your quest."

Sta nek, sensing that something important was happening between Tselique and Cha it zit, remained silent as he watched his wife fill the cooking box with spring water from a bucket she kept nearby. The rocks, he noted, were taking on a red-brown hue and would soon be ready to be dropped into the water along with a handful of dried nettle leaves.

"I feel tired...so tired," the old shaman said so all could hear. Others had gathered in the longhouse, elders who could no longer go on the food-gathering trips and those too young. They had kept a respectful distance so they seemed not to be intruding, but close enough to make their presence felt. "Now that it is over, I must rest." Tselique made an effort to rise but Tseutsi remonstrated.

"My brother-in-law," she said firmly, "yours has been an ordeal. We all know that. Stay and let this brew ease your stomach and refresh you. Then you may rest. Later, I will make a healing soup, easy for your body to accept—nourishing to build your strength. Once you are strong, you may do as you wish, but till then stay here with us, your people."

Tselique sank back upon the mat. "You are a good woman. My brother did well when he married you," he said, "I will do as you say, but my very bones are tired. Already I feel the presence of the spirit that will guide me to the land of the dead beneath us."

"Hush," Tseutsi flung at him, "do not talk so. Even you should not speak in such a way."

The woman turned to her fire. With split-maple tongs she angrily snared a hot rock and dropped it, hissing, into the cooking box, then another and another until the water simmered and steamed. Then she tossed in the dried nettles to steep. Soon, she passed a ladle of the aromatic brew to Tselique, who drank deeply, then to her husband, and last to Cha it zit. The hot drink soothed the youth's aching belly and numbed his mind. Suddenly, he wanted to sleep. Tselique noticed the drooping boy.

"He needs sleep even more than food," he said.

"Let him sleep, then, and you too. I will wake you when the soup is ready," Tseutsi agreed.

Both of them laid down on the mats and soon a sleep that was like death itself came upon them.

Cha it zit awoke, coming out of his sleep slowly, when he felt the pressure of a hand on his head.

"It is ready," his grandfather was saying. "come and eat. You need food."

When the boy's vision cleared, he saw that Sta nek was kneeling beside him, a bowl filled with steaming chowder in his hands. "Eat it all, but slowly," he told Cha it zit, "so your belly will accept it."

Cha it zit took the soup and sipped its nourishing goodness. He noticed that Tselique was doing likewise, under the stern scrutiny of Tseutsi.

The days went by. Cha it zit gained his strength rapidly, but Tselique did so at a much slower rate. It seemed that his body would not respond in spite of the care and concern lavished on him.

No one asked him about his spirit quest, which bothered Cha it zit. He really wanted to talk about it. He wanted to tell how he had felt, what happened — and then he remembered Tselique's warning, and so he, too, avoided the subject.

As he grew stronger, Cha it zit began to help around the longhouse. He carried water from the spring even though it was considered to be girl's work. He brought in firewood for Tseutsi and even watched the young children

to give the elders a rest. He helped Sta nek fashion fish-hooks and weave nets from cedarbark twine and often took his small canoe into the bay to catch fresh fish for those who had remained in the village.

His song had left him. It no longer pounded in his head as it had when it first came to him. He worried that the Tiolbax spirit had left him, too. He knew that a time of testing lay ahead, but that wouldn't be until the winter feasts, the time when the spirits came and possessed those who had earned them. Cha it zit thought of that time constantly, both in anticipation and in dread.

That was when he would have to prove his power. To fail could mean expulsion from the village and it would certainly mean disgracing himself and his family.

He worried about Tselique, too. Cha it zit saw that the old shaman had retreated into himself, not communicating with anyone. For long periods Tselique disappeared. No one knew where he went or what he did. Cha it zit wanted — longed — to talk to him, to tell him of the longhouse under the sea, of the voice that had spoken, but there was no opportunity.

The summer was turning into autumn. Soon the ducks would fly north and the villagers would return. There was excitement in the air. The old people cleaned and swept the interiors of the great houses. Room must be made to store the boxes of prepared food that the gatherers would bring back with them. New mats were made to replace the old frayed ones that hung all along the inside walls, insulation against the cold winter winds soon to come. Baskets and storage boxes had to be made and repaired so that they could be filled.

Each day watchers scanned the water for the first sight of returning canoes, and each day the people would say, "Maybe tomorrow."

Cha it zit was busy from dawn to dusk. It seemed that the children were too small and the elders too old, so he was called upon to do all the heavy tasks. "Cha it zit, bring me some water," or "I need wood for my fire," or "Help me strip these cattails," or "Carry this load, my back is breaking." He did it all without complaint, for there was no one else to do it.

Then one day the call came. "Canoes — they are coming." Everyone ran, was carried, or tottered down to the beach. Laughing, waving, shouting, they welcomed family members home. Everyone, that is, except Cha it zit.

He stood on the rise above the water where he could best see the approaching canoes. The dots grew larger until at last he spotted the one carrying Latsi, Wanana and Sax ump ki leading the rest. It seemed to the boy that it had been a lifetime since he had last seen them. Latsi was looking for him, he knew. He waved from his perch on the small rise and soon he saw Latsi wave back. He saw her motion to his mother and she looked but did not wave. Sax ump ki, busy with his paddle, did not look up.

"No matter," Cha it zit thought happily, his father would be relieved that he was safe and soon he would know that the quest had been successful. "And mother," he smiled inwardly, "she could drop this pose of distance once she knew he had proved himself...and Latsi, how good it would be to see her again."

He raced down the slope toward the beach and splashed out into the water. The canoe was nearing rapidly, but not fast enough for Cha it zit. He was shoulder-deep in the water when he grabbed the prow and tugged the canoe, occupants and all, toward the beach. Latsi jumped into the water beside him and, laughing, they raced to the shore, pulling the anchor line. When the canoe was secured, Cha it zit returned to help unload the supplies they had brought back.

Wanana's face gleamed with happiness when she saw her son alive and well. She longed to hold him, as she had when he was little, but she spoke, instead, in a reserved manner befitting the relationship between a man-son and his mother.

"My son," she said, "I am pleased to see you."

Cha it zit rejoiced. "She spoke to me. My mother spoke to me," he sang inside himself. Outwardly, he said, "I am also pleased to see you, my mother."

Sax ump ki approached his son, laid a hand on his shoulder and looked into his eyes. "I am grateful to see you here. I feel that you have succeeded in that which you set out to do. We will not speak of it now — there is much work to be done, but when the time is right, we will talk together, you and I."

Nothing more was said.

The days came, were filled with activity, and passed. So much needed to be accomplished before the darkness and the rains came. All the foods that had been gathered and dried — clams, fish, venison, roots, berries, seaweeds, and camas were stored away. Groups left the village to paddle and pole up the great river to the mountain country. There the women gathered huckle- and blueberries while the hunters sought bear, deer, and elk. Wool from mountain goats was gathered from bushes where it had snagged as the herd passed by. Always they remained alert, listening and watching for supernatural beings that were known to inhabit the deep forests and mighty mountains. They were in alien country where dangers lurked. It was only the *spirit power* of the hunters which kept them safe, they reasoned.

Those who remained behind performed countless tasks. Fishermen added to the stores already stacked in baskets and boxes on shelves in the houses. Women turned to basket making, drawing on materials they had gathered during respites from food processing. They knew that many baskets would be needed for the winter feasts. Artisans worked on trays and utensils. Children ran errands, old people tended babies and the cooking fires.

Of all the people, no one was busier than Cha it zit. He hunted with his father and Cha wentz, learning to stalk and kill, and then to butcher and bring his meat home in manageable bundles. He learned to fashion bow and arrow and to shoot with accuracy. He helped his grandfather fashion lures and hooks for halibut and then to use them to snare the wily fish.

Never once did he speak of his quest, but his mind was constantly occupied with the true meaning of the words he had heard. "What is my power?" he wondered. "When will I know what it will do for me ?"

One evening, when the family had finished the evening meal and were resting on their mats in the darkened house with only the glow of the fires giving light, Sax ump ki rose from his place and tapped his talking stick sharply. The people roused themselves to hear what he had to say.

"We have come to the end of our labors," he began. "The seas have been good to us. Our storage boxes are full. Now the wind blows cold, the days are short, soon we will feel the spirits returning to us, to possess our bodies, to give us power. It is time to tend to their needs, as well as to our own." The chief paused for a few moments and then continued. "You know that Cha it zit, my son, has undertaken his spirit quest. He must have the opportunity to prove that quest — to show what his power can do. Soon he will join the spirit dances. If his quest was a true one, we shall know."

Cha it zit listened and his emotions startled him. He felt both fear and joy. Fear of the torment and of failure. Suppose he had not had a true vision after all? Joy that soon he would know.

"Now," Sax ump ki continued, "we must prepare for a second feast for Cha it zit so that he may be properly acknowledged. His time of testing draws near."

And so the preparations began. This was to be a clan gathering. Only related families were invited, those who shared a common heritage.

"For this we must erect a special smokehouse," Sax ump ki directed. So men were sent to bring back cedar logs to build the frame and to split boards for the sides. The work was hard, and with the growing cold and frequent rains, it was unpleasant. Cha it zit helped, smoothing boards with a jade adz until his hands blistered and then bled. When the boards had been tied in place and shakes had been placed on the sloping roof and the building was finished Sax ump ki smiled in pleasure and said, "We are ready."

The spirits began to return. Men fell ill, their bodies resisting the spirits, and were relieved only when their spirit songs came to them and they could sing them. The people were careful where they walked, who they associated with, what they said, lest their souls be snatched by an errant force. Certain foods were avoided because they were offensive to the spirits. Strange things happened. Life became increasingly precarious as the spirits took possession of the village.

Cha it zit was acutely aware of all of this, but his spirit, Tiolbax, made no appearance. He felt no force in him. Even the song, which he had sung so freely after the vision, failed to come to him. He worried. Then he felt a deep urge to talk to Tselique.

Thinking of the old shaman, Cha it zit realized that he hadn't seen him for a number of days. The hours had been so filled with endless duties that there had been no time to think of Tselique, how he was feeling, what he was doing. So the boy went to find him. "Where is Tselique?" he asked his grandfather. "I must talk to him."

"I have not seen him for many days."

"Did he tell you that he was going somewhere?"

"No," Sta nek answered shaking his head until the greying hair was in disarray, "Tselique...he was not well...ask your grandmother, she hovers over him like a hen duck over her young."

When he asked Tseutsi she looked worried. "I do not know. He just faded away. Poof! He was gone. Find him," she ordered, "he is old. His strength is failing. Bring him here so I can care for him."

Tselique was not in the village. No one had seen him. Then Cha it zit remembered the island where he had first met the shaman. The day was wearing on and the sky was black and threatening, but the boy launched his canoe and headed for the open water.

Cha it zit had learned the ways of the sea. Since that first trip, during his period of training when Sax ump ki had sent him out, he had become an excellent paddler. Now he was the master of his light craft, it obeyed him.

There was no fear in Cha it zit. Born to the water, it was his environment, safer, by far, than the dark forests of the land.

His strong arms sent the canoe over the water swiftly. Not even the rising waves, now bristling with windblown spray, could deter him. Before darkness — total starless darkness — overtook him he beached his canoe on the shore of the island and called out, "Tselique! It is me, Cha it zit."

Only the wind answered him.

Then he followed the faint path and came to the ancient longhouse. Inside, by the last light of the day, he saw the fur rug move.

"Tselique!" he called again. "It is me, Cha it zit."

"I knew you would come," Tselique answered in a hoarse voice. "I willed you to come." The figure tried to sit up, coughed, and sank back down into the fur.

"Do you want water?" Cha it zit asked, fear in his voice. "He can't die...he can't die," he said to himself.

"Bring some. A spring..." the old man pointed a bony finger.

The boy found an ancient wooden bucket and left the longhouse, following a barely visible trail in the direction Tselique had indicated. Soon he heard the soft voice of a brook bubbling out of the ground. The water smelled sweet. Cha it zit laid full length on the ground, drank of the water and splashed some on his body. Then he filled the bucket and hurried back, retracing his steps in the dim light.

Lifting Tselique's head, he gave him a drink from a ladle which had been lying near the bucket. The old man sipped slowly and seemed to gain strength.

"It is good," he said huskily, "a gift to all things."

"Now you must eat," Cha it zit told him, imitating Tseutsi.

"There is no food," Tselique told him. "I had no energy. Once I got here I was exhausted."

"Then I will get some. There must be clams on the beach." Cha it zit left the house. It was nearly dark and he had to feel his way along the narrow path. Out in the open, the beach became visible, though barely. Using his hands, he dug into the sandy gravel, groping for the sweet steamer clams that lay just under the surface. It was difficult work, separating the clams from the gravel, but he worked with determination. As he labored, he thought how glad he was for the time he had spent with the elders during the summer. He could dig clams as well as a woman, and he knew how to cook them, too. "Clam soup could save Tselique's life," he realized.

The rich chowder, slowly spooned into Tselique's mouth, was truly a bringer of life. Soon the old man drifted off into a deep sleep and Cha it zit sat alone beside the fire he had built.

In the morning Tselique woke to the rays of the rising sun. They shone through the broken roof, bathing the emaciated old body in a soft warmth. Cha it zit was sitting beside him. "Ah," Tselique said, "we must talk. I was afraid I had waited too long, but you, my nephew, have given me the strength."

"Do not tire yourself," Cha it zit answered. "Once you are well we can talk. And then I will take you back with me. I will need your help for the trial I must undergo. It will be soon."

"Yes...yes, I know. That is why I must speak to you now."

Tselique pulled himself into a sitting position. "Ah! that is better. My body is frail. It is too frail to hold the spirit of a shaman. It will soon leave me. Even now it is looking for a body worthy to receive it. I grow weak. You grow strong. For a long time, now, I have known that my power is drawn to you. Whether you choose it or not, it will come to you. You must learn how to use it, how to handle it."

"But my power is...."

"Stop. Do not use the name. I know of your vision, yes, I know of your power. But that will not change things. You are strong—you will stand the presence of two spirits. Together they will make you a great leader, wealthy and respected. Cha it zit, you will be a shaman...and you will be much more."

"It is not my wish," the boy said.

"The spirit which I possess has decided. It is not for you to choose."

"What is this spirit? How will I know it?"

"You have seen the raven many times. That is its outward appearance. Its real shape remains secret. Its magical powers are felt, not seen."

"The raven," Cha it zit said, wonder in his voice. "It followed me when I first began my training, when I deposited the stick. I have seen it many times, it even appeared when I sought my spirit gift, flying over the open water."

"Yes, it has always been near you."

"You sent it? You knew?"

"Yes," Tselique replied. "I knew."

"Why me? You have other grand-nephews, older and braver than I am...Cha wentz, for one."

"You are of my blood—and of my heart. Now I have things to tell you. Listen and remember, for when the time comes this knowledge will be important."

"I will remember."

"Do you see the bentwood box in the corner?" Tselique waved a forefinger toward a distant part of the house. "Bring it to me."

Cha it zit hastened to obey.

Tselique opened the box and took out a painted board, faded with age. He held it up for the boy to see. Its design was strange, a white background with black dots arranged in the figure of a bird.

"This spirit board, and the others like it, still in the box, have protected me on visits to the land of the dead. It was my uncle's before me. Its power is great. Tselique jerked the board from Cha it zit's curious fingers. "Do not touch it now. You will know when the time is right, the time when it will be yours to use."

"How is it used?"

"Let me explain," Tselique offered. "One of a powerful shaman's tasks is to find souls that have become lost or stolen and have been taken to the land of the dead. It requires great power to retrieve lost souls, and it is dangerous, but necessary to save the life of one whose soul is gone.

"First, when I was able to perform this feat, I called upon my spirit power. When it came into me I went into a trance. My own soul went forth out of my body, and with the help of these spirit boards which I had placed about me in the shape of a canoe, I began a journey to the land of the dead in search of the lost soul. It was dangerous.

"I passed many terrifying beings and faced many challenges. At any time, if my power was not strong enough, I could be lost there forever. When, at last, I reached the land of the dead, I entered the village to search for the lost soul. When I found it, I used my *soul catcher*."

Tselique reached into the box and extracted a small, carved bone with an opening at each end. "This," he said, "is capable of snatching a soul and of holding

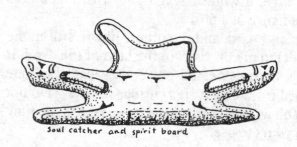

Soul catcher and spirit board

138

it. The trip back was easier and safer than going, for I then knew the way."

Cha it zit listened, his eyes wide with wonder, his mind imagining the experiences Tselique encountered.

"When I returned, I would place the soul catcher to the patient's chest and blow through one side of it, blowing the lost soul back into him."

"You did that?" Cha it zit's voice was filled with amazement.

"Many times. Did no one tell you of it?"

"No one."

"Children are protected from those things. Their souls are known to be very unstable. That is why you did not know." Tselique explained. "Even now, when you are a man-boy, it is not wise to speak of such spiritual things. But I must. They must be made known to you."

"Will I be able to do as you did?"

Tselique smiled. "Not now...it takes time and dedication to build such power. You may not use your power for a long time. First, you must grow and mature. But someday it will become so strong, so insistent that you must use it."

"What else did you do?"

"I healed by finding the evil thing that caused the sickness and then extracting it from the body."

"What sort of thing?"

"Horrible, worm-like, slimy things."

"Ugh," Cha it zit shuddered.

"Yes, unpleasant, but how good to be able to remove them." Tselique, thoroughly caught up in the recital continued, "If I were to harm a man, I could do so without touching him."

"How?"

"Give me the bag that I usually wear around my neck. It is in the box, too."

Cha it zit found the worn, age-darkened leather pouch and handed it to Tselique.

"In here are many charms...bits of bones and dried herbs. Each has its use, with them I worked my magic.

"It is not for you to know how I did it. Each shaman creates his own charms, his own *squidelich*."

The two of them talked for many hours. Tselique told Cha it zit secrets that had been known to shamen of his family for countless generations. The boy's mind reeled as the information was unfolded to him.

At last Tselique said, "It is done. Now I instruct you to remember all that I told you.

"When I am gone, interred in the manner of shaman, you are to take the box and keep it. The day will come when you will use it. Use it wisely. The power in it is great, just as the spirit power which will come to you is great."

"I must leave," Cha it zit told Tselique on the morning after their talk. "Come with me. Grandmother will tend to your needs, and grandfather wishes to see you."

"You have given me strength," Tselique answered, "I will stay here. When your time of trial comes, I will be there."

When Cha it zit returned to the village he found that arrangements had been made for the feast and dances when he would be expected to prove his spirit power.

"In seven days," his grandfather told him, "our guests will arrive. I suggest you prepare yourself so that you do not bring shame upon us, your family or upon you."

"Prepare myself? How?"

"Most do it by spending time alone in the forest, and by cleansing and fasting. Those things please the spirits and prevent other forces from interfering. The spirits do not like human scent, so we bathe, they do not like certain foods, so we avoid them, they do not like strong emotions, so we control our bodies and our thoughts."

"So I must isolate myself and undergo privation until the time comes. Is that what you are saying?"

"We will set apart a place for you in the longhouse, or you may find your own spot. Cha wentz will act as a communicator for you. He will tell you when you are to appear and what you are to do."

"My brother and I are not the same. He is a warrior, with a warrior spirit. How can he advise me? I have a different gift."

"That is how it will be," Sta nek said as he turned his back on Cha it zit and walked away.

Latsi had been listening. She slipped out from behind a stack of storage boxes where she had been hiding.

"Oogli," she whispered, using his old pet name. "I'll come with you if you go into the woods. I can cook for you."

"Latsi," his voice showed surprise, dismay, and affection all at the same time. "You shouldn't be spying like that."

"I wasn't spying," she answered indignantly, "I just happened to be there. Besides, I care."

"But I have to do this alone. What would people say if my sister came with me? What would my spirit helper think? It might think I was a weakling and leave me altogether."

"Where will you go?" Latsi asked, concern in her voice. "Maybe you should just stay here in a secret place, like grandfather said you could. Then I could whisper to you what is happening."

"Cha wentz can do that. No, Latsi, it is not right for you to be part of this. Go and help Mother. What I must do is man's business."

Latsi looked long and hard at her brother. Hurt showed in her face, and then her eyes narrowed and hardened with a new understanding and she left him.

Cha it zit walked to the spot above the beach where he always went to ponder a problem or just to dream. Before long he was joined by Cha wentz.

"Brother, I have been asked to assist you," he announced tersely.

"I know, grandfather told me," Cha it zit answered in a flat tone, showing no enthusiasm for the turn of events.

"Where will you go? I must know."

"I have been thinking about that. There is a small lake, near the bend of the river. Do you know the place?"

"Yes, I have hunted ducks there."

"That is where I will be." Chat it zit announced, surprised at his own statement. He had made the decision without any forethought.

The two brothers sat together. Neither could think of anything to say — the gap between them was too great. At last Cha wentz rose to go.

"I will see you at the lake," he said.

The lake was marshy so Cha it zit set up his camp on high ground some distance back from the water. He built a lean-to of poles and covered it with cattail mats that Wanana had provided. With a small fire burning at the front, the shelter was comfortable enough, but the rains sent rivulets of water running across the ground and the wind blew smoke back into the living space.

In spite of the difficulties, the time went quickly. The raven arrived soon after Cha it zit had set up his camp and never left except to forage for food. There was an abundance of game and roots to dig, so, although he was careful not to eat strong-tasting foods, the boy did not go hungry.

He dug the fat, starchy roots of cattails out of the swampy edges of the lake, using his strong toes. Then he roasted them in coals until they were tender. He treated the roots of water lilies that grew in profusion the same way. He caught perch and trout on hooks that he had fashioned of small cedar boughs, steaming and bending the wood into a hook-like shape. For line, he twisted nettle stems into stout cords. Salmon and ducks, Cha it zit avoided, although he could easily have netted them along the river, for they were strong foods and could upset the spirit powers.

The weather was unpleasant. A heavy drizzle wet him and the cold air penetrated to his very bones, but he had long ago learned to endure, and if possible, to overcome his own weaknesses.

To keep track of the days, he knotted a leather thong each time the sun rose in the grey, watery sky. When he had tied the sixth knot the reality came to him that the Tiolbax spirit had not appeared, or even made its presence felt. This caused Cha it zit deep concern.

"Could it be that I only dreamed the *vision*?" he wondered. "No, that could not be so," he quickly countered the thought. "It was so real." The terrible possibility, with all of its implications remained. He could not put it behind him. The absolute disgrace of it, not only to him, but to his entire family made the thought totally unacceptable.

He called out loud, "Spirit...Tiolbax," only to be answered by the cawing of the raven.

"Tselique," he called again. "I need your help." Again the raven answered, swooping low and up again to perch on a nearby tree bough.

"You, Raven," Cha it zit called, "You and Tselique are as one. Help me!" The raven called out three times and flew off.

Cha it zit was deserted. What would he do, he wondered. If he tried, as others had done, to fake a vision and spirit powers, he would soon be found out. No, the only thing possible was to wait and hope that when he needed it the Tiolbax would make itself felt. And so he waited beside his fire for whatever fate had in store for him.

Some time later he heard his name being called. He answered and Cha wentz appeared.

"It is time," he said. "Everyone is gathered in the new smokehouse built for you for this occasion. I have been sent to bring you. We must hurry, it will be getting dark."

"Cha wentz," Cha it zit cried in a panic, "I can't come. All this time I have had no sign that my spirit power is real. I am afraid to come."

Cha wentz's face went dark with scorn. "You must come," he told Cha it zit. "Now, listen to me."

The two sat down by the fire and the older brother spoke at first scathingly, and then his tone softened as he realized the seriousness of the situation for Cha it zit.

"The people have been evoking their spirits and the dances are beginning. There will be much power present tonight—strange unspeakable things will happen," Cha wentz said. "Perhaps your power will come, too. Perhaps the drums and the dances will bring it. Now, to make it really happen you must be daring and courageous. Put the fear that you feel behind you. Can you do that?"

"I will try."

"This is what we must do. I will run in the door shouting that you are coming. You climb up on the roof, and when you hear my voice, leap through the smokey hole. Shout and throw yourself about like a mad man. I've seen it happen like that."

"But," Cha it zit objected, "with the fire underneath, I'll jump right into the fire. You know how big and hot they build the smokehouse fires." The boy was appalled at the prospect.

"No, move quickly, or try for the side. Anyway, what's a burn if it brings you the power you want?"

"If it is the only way," Cha it zit said doubtfully. "You will be there. Grab me if I don't move fast enough or if I fall into the fire."

"I'll be there," Cha wentz answered. For the first time in their lives the brothers felt close. It was a good feeling, and it warmed Cha it zit. He began to feel as if there might be a gleam of hope for him in the ordeal he was about to undertake.

By the time the two arrived at the smokehouse the night, ink-black, had settled over the village. The drums were beating a persistent, hypnotic thunder.

"Now." Cha wentz ordered. "Up on the roof. When you hear me yell, 'He is coming!' jump through the smoke hole."

Propelled by some inner force, Cha it zit scrambled up a supporting post and poised beside the smoke hole which was spewing forth a fiery column of thick, resinous smoke.

Suddenly the drums stopped and he heard "He is coming...he is here!"

Down through the hole Cha it zit plunged and landed in flowing coals fifteen feet below. A reflex action bounced him back to the earthen floor, and he felt no pain. Then, without knowing why he began to scream like one gone mad. His body contorted and the cry that came from his throat was like the call of a raven. The drums began to beat, softly, persistently as he moved, and the cry became a song. It wavered uncertainly in his throat and emerged.

> "I saw it, I saw it.
> I found it, I found it
> its power is great
> it is mine, it is mine"

The drums picked up the tempo, tentatively and then surely, and Cha it zit's voice was heard above it all.

Round and round he danced in a peculiar, mincing step, his arms flapping like wings. The drums beat into his brain, they dominated his body, propelling him on and on until he lost his grasp of reality. Nothing existed for him save the drums, the song, and the dance.

Then he saw it. In the smoke of the fire he saw a figure. Slowly it emerged and he knew that it was Tselique, standing in the fire. Raising a bony arm, the old shaman beckoned to him. Cha it zit danced closer, answering in a raven's cry. Closer and closer, Cha it zit danced until his feet touched the glowing coals. On he went, obeying the compelling gesture of Tselique. As the boy advanced, the shaman retreated. Through the fire the boy danced, and when he reached the other side he dropped to the floor, exhausted and unconscious.

Slowly, as in a dream, Cha it zit's senses returned. First it was the persistent beating of the drums that penetrated the numbness of his brain. Then the voices of the people added to the din. Over and over they were singing a spirit song—his song. Then he felt, rather than saw, the close presence of his father.

"Where is he?" Cha it zit asked, his voice thick and hoarse.

"Where is who?" Sax ump ki wondered.

"Tselique."

"He is not here. I have not seen him for many days."

"I saw him. He was in the fire. He promised he would come and he did. I saw him." Cha it zit persisted.

"In the fire?" Sax ump ki asked in amazement.

"It was he who bade me dance through the fire to him."

"It was your spirit that you saw. That was a powerful thing that you did." Sax ump ki's voice betrayed the pride that he felt. "Tonight you have proven your gift. Only a man with a very strong *gift* could do a thing like that. A shaman's gift, perhaps."

"No!" Cha it zit spat out the refusal. "That is not the spirit that I found, that promised to help me. I will not have

146

a shaman spirit. My spirit is one that will bring me power and wealth."

"Be careful, my son," Sax ump ki cautioned. "Spirit helpers must be treated with care or they can turn against you. I tell you, you have found a shaman spirit, or perhaps it has found you. However it is, you must accept it. Many shaman become rich and powerful. You will, too, for you have a strong spirit. But enough of this talk. You have honored this family. Your quest has been successful, we all know, and you will take your place among us. I am content."

Sax ump ki stood up and motioned Cha it zit to rise. Shakily the boy pulled himself erect and stood by his father.

When the drummers saw their host standing with Cha it zit beside him they beat a flurry, softened, and then the room was quiet. All eyes were focused on the pair.

"My people," Sax ump ki began, "you have seen that Cha it zit has proven that he has received a great gift, a true gift. He will take his place in this village and will be respected by all the clans. I ask that you remember this night." The people murmured their approval and then Sta nek rose from his place on the platform. He rapped sharply with his talking stick.

"I, too, ask that you remember what Cha it zit, my grandson, has done. He has brought honor on this house. The spirits are here, I feel them all around us. Let the drums talk. Let the power be felt. Let the dances and the songs come out."

Through the long winter night the dancers rose and performed their spirit dances. Round the fire they careened and pranced, letting their spirit powers propel them until they dropped from exhaustion.

Toward morning the drums became mute and the people wrapped themselves in blankets and slept.

Shaman's Rattle

The Spirit Speaks

The morning came, though it scarcely seemed different from the night. A pale sun shone through a slate-grey sky reflecting on slate-grey water. There was moisture in the air, not truly rain, more a wet towel hanging over everything. Spider webs ornamenting trees and shrubs were hung with pearls of dew. Not even the seabirds were flying on this dull day.

The people in the longhouse began to stir. Women replenished the dying fires and brought out food baskets. Children snuggled deeper into blankets of mountain goat wool and bear skins while young men sauntered to the beach to bathe in the icy waters.

It was the old men who urged action upon the group. They prodded the wives to hurry with breakfast and once they had eaten they began to lay out boards and mats. Cha it zit watched the preparations with interest.

He knew that they were preparing to play sla hal, the gambling game. It had fascinated him before, now the idea of actually playing the game himself intrigued him. Never had he dared ask if he could take part. Sla hal was only for the skilled, and besides, he had nothing to wager. Now that he had gained stature, it would be different, he thought. If he could just play, someone might place bets for him.

He watched as they brought out the counting sticks, eleven in all, and placed them in front of the boards which had been placed opposite each other about five feet apart. Then they laid beating sticks on the boards so that the players could beat to the ruthless rhythm of the sla hal song.

Soon others drifted to the area and took their places on the mats behind the boards. Two elders, chosen as team captains, sat in the center of each line of players, facing each other.

Then Cha it zit dared to speak. "I wish to play."

The gamblers smiled broadly, amused at his audacity. One captain said, "The boy is a man. He thinks he can play this game. Shall we see what he can do?"

Cha it zit held his breath while the players considered. Finally the other team captain said, "There is room for him on my team." Turning to Cha it zit he asked, "What do you have to bet?"

The boy waited before answering, hoping that someone would offer to bet for him, but no one spoke, so he finally replied, "I have the canoe my father gave to me."

"Done," the old man agreed.

Cha it zit took his place at one end of the board and picked up a beating stick. The song began and he sang too, beating on the board in a steady, strong tempo.

Each of the leaders displayed their playing bones. Cha it zit knew, from the many times he had watched the play, that each leader would guess for the plain bone. The banded bone was a losing guess. All of the guessing was done by gestures, timed to the beat of the sticks — a sort of dance, one that had been practiced until it was an art. With each correct guess a team received a counting stick. When one side had won all eleven, the game was over and the winning team took their gains.

The hiding of the bones, concealed in the leader's closed fists, the guessing for them by the opposite leader by gesture, began. On and on the game went. The counting sticks moved back and forth between the two teams. The hours went by, but Cha it zit was fascinated by the game and didn't notice.

Occasionally the leaders would toss the bones to a team member to hold while the opponent guessed. Suddenly, Cha it zit held the *bones* and he shook them as he had seen others do. Then he grasped them in his fists and extended both arms out and drew them back to his belly in the customary way.

His opponent guessed by slapping his chest in the time-honored way, and pointing to Cha it zit's right hand, forefinger lowered. Cha it zit opened his fist. The banded female bone lay in that hand, and a cue stick was passed to him.

He kept the bones, repeated the play and again his opponent guessed wrong. Another stick was laid with the first. Again and again the leader failed to guess the male bone. The pile of counters at Cha it zit's feet grew.

In his frustration, the leader designated another player to guess for him. He failed to turn the tide, and after one final guess all eleven sticks lay in a row, a victory for Cha it zit's side.

The beating stopped and the sla hal song died in the singers' throats. After the hours of monotonous, strident noise, the silence was shocking. The longhouse was dark, and Cha it zit realized that an entire day had passed. Only the ever-burning hearth fires lit the scene.

"What power do you have that the *bones* work for you?" the opposing leader called angrily to Cha it zit.

"Leave him alone," the leader of Cha it zit's team growled. "He has played well. It is not for you to question his powers, strong as they seem to be."

The two elders, both respected and known for their gambling successes, glared at each other. "That is well for you to say, since he won for you," the loser said. Then he turned to Cha it zit. "You may sit on my side any time you wish. A gift such as yours is welcome."

"I accepted him when his *gift* was not known," the other snarled. "His loyalty should be to me."

The winning players began to gather their newly gained wealth and the losers stalked off to solace themselves in another occupation—eating, story telling, reminiscing, or playing another less demanding game.

Cha it zit felt a hand on his shoulder and looked up into the smiling face of his sla hal leader. "It must be true that you have a *gift* for gambling. It will bring wealth to you. Today you have taken the first step toward that goal. Guard your *gift*, but use it too, make it work for you. Some day you will be a great and respected man. Your name will be known throughout all the villages. All the people will know the name, Cha it zit."

"Could it be?" the boy wondered as he smiled his appreciation for the old man's words. "Could it be that I have the Tiolbax spirit after all?

"But what of Tselique and the shaman spirit he said I would get?" The questions kept coming. "Where is Tselique? Why is he hiding from me? He said he would come...what has happened?"

He wanted to be alone to think, but he also desperately wanted to talk to Tselique. As Cha it zit always did when he had a problem, he went outside into the dusk and groped his way to his perch overlooking the beach.

The evening air felt cold and sweet on his body. A few stars were peeping out between unseen clouds. Below he could hear the quiet slap, slap of the waves as they churned onto the stony shore. Somewhere off across the water lay the island where he had first seen Tselique.

Then Cha it zit heard the raven caw. "Hey, Raven," he called, "You should be with Tselique...wherever he is." The bird answered with three caws, and was quiet.

Cha it zit felt refreshed. He wandered back to the longhouse.

The people were beginning to gather for the evening meal. Children, excited by the afternoon's games of hide and seek, tug-of-war, and races, ran in and out. Women opened food boxes, heated rocks and brought buckets of water to the fires. Men, lounging on mats at the fire's edges, watched the activity. Cha it zit knew that all of the activity was in his honor, to assure his place in the clan, but he felt detached — not really a part of it.

Then he saw Latsi helping his mother, and he realized that he hadn't had a talk with her for a long time — she who had been so big a part of his life was slipping away. During all the man-oriented functions Latsi had no place. "Not now," he thought, "but soon I must let her know that I haven't forgotten her, not Latsi."

Sta nek was sitting on a bentwood box at his place on the platform doing nothing in particular. He spied Cha it zit and beckoned to him. Obediently, the boy threaded his way through the groups of guests toward the far end of the longhouse. Then he mounted the platform and stood before his grandfather.

"Sit," the old man said, pointing to another box nearby. Cha it zit pulled the heavy box closer and sat upon it, waiting to hear the words that Sta nek would speak.

"You have done well. I am a proud man today. In you I see future greatness.

"I saw you leap fearlessly from the roof into the fire. You did not flinch. Your song came, and your dance. Your spirit power was strong — a true *gift*. I saw you walk through the hot coals. You showed no pain. Your feet, they are not burned?"

"No," answered the boy as he raised his feet to show the soles, calloused from running, but whole.

"That is good," the old man smiled. "No spirit but that of a shaman could do what you did. My brother Tselique spoke to me of it.

"His wish to give you his power was strong. It must be that his spirit was willing. That must be the way it is."

"But," Cha it zit fretted, "but I did not receive that gift on my quest. The gift I wanted was the one I found. I know because...."

The old man held up his hand. "Do not tell me. Remember to tell no one the nature of your gift. It is dangerous. A person who knows can harm you."

Cha it zit nodded and remained silent.

"Today you played sla hal," Sta nek changed the direction of their talk.

"Yes," the boy replied. "You know about it?"

"Everyone knows. It is the concern of the village. They say you have found a gambling spirit."

"What they say is true," Cha it zit said, simply.

"To have a shaman's power and a gambler's spirit at the same time, and in one so young is quite remarkable." Sta nek slapped his knee and chuckled at the thought of the possibilities.

"It is strange," Cha it zit admitted, "but it must be so."

"I know Tselique had something to do with it. Where is he? Do you know?" Cha it zit's tone was urgent.

154

Sta nek looked at him sharply. His eyes suddenly darkened as though some evil thought had intruded.

"I have not seen my brother for five days now," he answered in a guarded tone.

"I must find him," Cha it zit said in a clear, determined voice.

"When it is over. When your spirit power is recognized and accepted by this gathering of our people, we will go."

"You will come with me?"

"I have said."

After the evening meal had been eaten and the remains tossed to the dogs, Sax ump ki mounted the platform where Sta nek was already waiting. He rapped sharply with his talking stick and the guests quieted. They sat motionless waiting for the oration to come.

Cha it zit felt a surge of pride; how tall he was, how proud he looked. "My father is a remarkable man," he thought.

"I thank you for coming into my house," he began. "You have witnessed an important event. You have seen that my son, Cha it zit has become a man.

"He has received a true gift, and he has proven that gift in an outstanding fashion. I ask that you acknowledge him and his power."

The people spoke among themselves. Cha it zit, sitting in the darkness below the platform, saw the face of Cha wentz highlighted by the light of the fires. He was shocked and dismayed by the expression. He saw malice where he would have expected to see acceptance. He saw envy. Instinctively he knew that Cha wentz, by birth his brother, would never be by choice his friend.

"It is his warrior spirit," Cha it zit rationalized. "Warriors have mean spirits. It is not in them to take pleasure in another's success."

Then he heard his father say, "I give you my son, Cha it zit, who is now a man." Cha it zit rose and joined Sta nek and Sax ump ki on the platform.

Looking at the assemblage, he saw the one who had been his leader at the sla hal game stand up. "I can attest to the power possessed by Cha it zit. He is worthy." Others stood, too, to endorse the success of the boy's quest. Not a warrior rose, but Cha it zit did not care. He had not wanted a violent spirit, and he did not now want their support. Like all of the people, he feared the warriors.

When the last person had spoken Sax ump ki thanked them, and it was over.

The drums began to *talk* and the people felt their own spirits coming upon them. Then the dances began. Far into the night, as they were moved, the dancers gave their bodies to the power of their spirits. Cha it zit danced, too, to the song that had come to him the night before. He was accepted — a man among men, with a power of his own.

It was over.

10

The End
And The
Beginning

It was mid-morning the next day when
Sta nek and Cha it zit launched a canoe and
headed toward the island. Cha it zit, in the stern, propelled
the craft, while Sta nek, weak with age, added what help he
could. They did not talk. Each was deep in his own thoughts.

When, several hours later, they neared the island,
Sta nek spoke. "We must call upon all our power to protect
ourselves. We don't know what we will find here. My
brother did much that was supernatural."

"I know," Cha it zit answered, "but we have to find
him. He may need us." There was fear coupled with determination in his voice.

"True."

They came upon the rotting longhouse and peered
inside. There was no movement there. No sign of life.

"Tselique," Cha it zit called. The only answer was
his own voice echoing back to him.

Cautiously they entered. Sta nek walked to a pile of ancient fur robes and pulled them aside. There they found Tselique. He had been dead for several days.

"How could that be," Cha it zit cried out in despair and amazement. "I saw him when I was doing my spirit dance. He was there!"

"I know," Sta nek answered after a long pause. "He had much power."

"You knew?" Amazement sounded through Cha it zit's words.

"Yes. It was his ghost that you saw. He kept his promise to you. He was there when you needed him most."

"Now I must keep my promise to him." Cha it zit took the box containing the shaman's possessions and placed it outside the longhouse. "He told me these were to be mine...that I would get a shaman spirit."

"I know," Sta nek repeated. "I know more than you think. Hide the box until you are ready to use it. You will know when that time has come."

The pair stood silently, each immersed in his own thoughts, his own private grief. At last Sta nek spoke.

"We must wrap him and treat his body with respect. His ghost must not linger here in the land of the living. We must help him to leave us and travel the route he knows so well to the world of the dead. There he will remain with his ancestors, doing those things that were customary to him. Some day," the old man's voice broke, "someday I...and you, too...will see him there."

They washed the aged body, wrapped it in the old mats and placed it reverently on boards in a tree. Then they quietly left the island.

"It is as he wished it," Sta nek said as they slowly paddled back to the mainland.

"He knew," Cha it zit said, not so much to Sta nek as to the sea and the breeze and the sky. "He knew I was to be

a shaman, and he helped me prove it. I will honor him by achieving greatness."

"Yes," Sta nek replied looking across the water, his old eyes seeing a vision of the future.

Epilogue

There is much more to be written about the great chief of the Lummis, Cha it zit. In the annals of history he is known as a good friend of the white men who arrived in Puget Sound during his middle years.

With great skill and compassion he guided his people through the first contacts with Europeans. He brought the first white people to Bellingham Bay and cared for them until they were established.

He stood staunchly on the side of order and cooperation between the two cultures. Knowing that the old way of life was over for the Indian people, he signed the treaty that placed the Lummis on a reservation which included all of their villages.

He saw Christianity tear the old beliefs from his people, but he saw the benefits it had to offer and encouraged the missionary fathers who came.

His people changed, as he knew they must, but Cha it zit, himself, remained true to his own convictions. He was a man who stood with his feet in two cultures.